Build Your Superior Chinese Vocabulary

(I)

Concepts and Rules

Reveal the Reasons and Whys Behind the Words

Crack the Biggest Barrier in Learning Chinese

by Zhou Xiaogeng

Copyright © 2017 Zhou Xiaogeng All rights reserved

This Edition is created by DIGICUBIC
as a core product of
**New Craftsman
of Chinese Language and Culture**
中国语言文化新工匠计划

PRODUCER: ZHOU XIAOGENG
DEVELOPER: DIGICUBIC
CHEIF EDITOR: ZHOU FURONG
ENGLISH EDITOR: Nicole Dentremont
ART ADMINISTRATOR: ZOEY.CHANG
RESOURCE SUPPORT: XUE XIULAN
PICUTURE: WWW.CHINAND.COM
DESIGNER: DIGICUBIC

出品人：周晓更
开发机构：数版立方
中文审校：周富荣
英文审校：NICOLE
艺术指导：ZOEY.CHANG
资源支持：薛秀兰
图库支持：WWW.CHINAND.COM
版式设计：数版立方

ISBN-13:9781548177355
ISBN-10:1548177350

About This Book

In case you want to have a fun chat with the Chinese Aunties (中国大妈 zhōngguó dà mā), or to engage a beautiful girl (or a charming man)sitting next to your table in a cafe, or to expand a grand business plan to your Chinese business partners, the first thing you need to do is to increase your vocabulary.

If it is a real headache for you to grasp thousands of words, you will find this book to be a magic antidote. In an intuitive and fun way, this book reveals the unique method of how this ancient language built up its vocabulary palace, and what's more important, it helps you to understand the ways of thinking and reasons for creating such a vast language. Finally you will find that Chinese is not a difficult language, it is just different.

Also, in order to make this book more helpful for solving some "realistic" language problems, such as, to help you to pass tests such as the HSK, BCT or final exam in your class, most of the example words in this book are selected from those words required by these various tests, or those most frequently used in everyday language.

As the first and fundamental book in Xiaogeng's Grammar Series, it focuses on something more general and basic of the Chinese vocabulary system. Also, you will find other books introducing specific types of words such like nouns, verbs, adverbs, prepositions, etc.

CONTENTS

001 Invisible Ties   *About Mandarin Chinese*   1

You probably may not have realized that, in fact, the Chinese language (汉语 hàn yǔ), which is also frequently called 中文 (zhōng wén), is completely different to that of Mandarin Chinese (普通话 pǔ tōng huà). It may surprise you even more that...

002 Immortal Bricks   *Chinese Characters*   9

Many learners have experienced this form of teaching: While the teacher is trying to explain some basic knowledge about Chinese characters, he or she would show how Chinese people create the character 日 (rì, sun; day) like creating a sketch painting...

003 Origin of the Legend   *Characters and Words*   17

In Mandarin Chinese, there are hundreds of polyphonic characters, and a few of them even have three or more pronunciations. You might have a question like this: Why did Chinese people create so many characters like thatunderstanding and using? ...

004 Infinite Possibilities   *Features of Vocabulary System*   27

If you happen to have both an English dictionary and a Chinese dictionary, compare them and you will find some interesting differences in them. In the English dictionary, each of the words appear as an independent term and is listed in a linear way...

005 Behind the Curtain   *Mechanism of Generating Vocabulary*   35

The method for words-creation in the Chinese language is easy to understand. Think about what you would do when you are trying to find something on an on-line shopping website: You will input several keywords and then will find a list suggested...

006 Ways of Nature   *Three Basic Meaning-Generating Types   43*

Don't think that we are going into some profound theories, on the contrary, everything that happens in the meaning-generating course is in accordance to common sense in our everyday life. The following examples will help you to understand...

007 It Makes Sense   *The Principle of "Rationality"   51*

Undoubtedly, the combining method brings unlimited possibilities in creating "new" words for this language. However, a coin always has two sides. A potential problem with this method is that it might generate excessive words if used without control...

008 The Hidden Center   *The Principle of "Core-in-End"   57*

In a specific combining course, the origin word referring to the essential features is called the "Core Word". In the above example, jī(机 machine; vehicle) is the core word because it describes the essential feature of the complicated machinery...

009 Stages of Growth   *The Principle of "One-off Functioning"   61*

Using the combining method, Chinese people can create unlimited basic words with limited characters (origin words). Meanwhile, people should still control the side-effect of the method; creating too many words. Too many words will also....

010 Blurry Borderlines   *Basic Words, Complex Words, and Phrases   67*

These words that refer to the elementary objects and concepts are called "Basic Words". In English, you can easily figure them out because they are listed as independent terms in a dictionary, with specific and unique appearances, definitions, and...

Copyright Statement

The sole author of this book is Zhou Xiaogeng, holding the exclusive and full copyrights of this entire book, including (but not limited to) the text, pictures, charts, etc....

This Edition is created by **DIGICUBIC** as a core product of
New Craftsman of Chinese Language and Culture
中国语言文化新工匠计划

If you need to quote (or in any manner use) the contents of this book, you should perform this action in a legal, reasonable, and bona fide way. If improper application of usage brings any harm or loss to a third party, the author is free of any and all responsibility. If the improper behavior of the user, such as illegal copying, plagiarism, illegal distribution, etc..., brings any harm or loss to the author, the author reserves the right to take legal action.

For detailed information and relative resources, please visit
www.chinand.com

In case you are interested in publishing this book in other language editions, or in developing the derived products, including unbounded online lectures, MOOCs, games, or in establishing co-operations with the author, please contact:
digicubic@126.com

001

Invisible Ties

About Mandarin Chinese

You probably may not have realized that, in fact, the Chinese language (汉语 hàn yǔ), which is also frequently called 中文 (zhōng wén), is completely different to that of Mandarin Chinese (普通话 pǔ tōng huà). It may surprise you even more that as far back as about seventy years ago, there was no Mandarin Chinese in the world at all!

The concept for the Chinese language is quite general and vague. As you know, there are about 1.4 billion people in China composed of 56 different ethnicities, among which the Ethnic of Han (汉族 hàn zú) make up more than 95% of the population. Generally speaking, the Chinese language can be regarded as the mother language of all the people from the Ethnic of Han. But you should know that, in many cases, many of the other ethnicities in China also have their own mother languages. For example, the native residents in Tibet (西藏, Xī zàng) speak Tibetan (藏语, zàng yǔ), which is a completely different language than the Chinese language.

Of the vast amount of people that speak the Chinese language, there are tens of local dialects that are also popularly used every day. For example, the native residents in Shanghai (上海 Shàng hǎi) usually speak Shanghainese, which is a dialect of the Chinese language, to each other, and the same situation happens in Guangzhou (广州 Guǎngzhōu), Chengdu (成都 Chéng dū), and many other regions.

It is interesting that some Chinese dialects are so different to each other that native speakers cannot even understand each other at all! Don't feel dismayed that a native Shanghainese speaker cannot understand a native Cantonese speaker. However, it is totally unacceptable that people living in a same country cannot fully understand each other because it will block the developing of the whole nation. An ultimate solution is to "create" an official language for all the civilians, and require everyone to speak it. That is why Mandarin Chinese was created.

To put it simply, Mandarin Chinese is a man-made language. It is based on the dialects near Beijing, and was then modified to be the standard official language. If you happen to visit the Jin Shan Ling Great Wall, you will find that the village beside it is proclaimed as the Origin of Mandarin Chinese.

What happens in my home reflects the typical situation of how Chinese people are using languages. When I speak to my mother, I prefer to speak the dialects of my hometown because it makes us feel more natural and comfortable. When I speak to my wife, my son, and my father, I speak Mandarin Chinese because they cannot speak the dialect of my hometown. As a guy born in northern China, I cannot understand many Chinese dialects of southern China, including Shanghainese and Cantonese. Thus, when I speak to people from southern China, we all speak Mandarin Chinese. When I am with friends from India and France, we all speak English. These situations may seem to be a little complicated, but it is natural in many places.

This is the Information Service Spot located in the Beijing West Railway Station (北京西站 běi jīng xī zhàn).

WORDS BANK

The following are top 10 most frequently used Chinese characters and the relative words that frequently appear in Chinese language tests.

Top One: 的 (de)

This character is frequently used to create some "temporary" words, and the typical applications are:

1. To indicate the possession by someone. Example:

   nǐ (你 you) + de (的) = nǐ de (你的 your; yours)

   nǐmen (你们 you (pl)) + de (的) = nǐ men de (你们的 your; yours (pl))

2. To build up phrases and to indicate the relation of the words inside. Example:

   Běi jīng (北京 Beijing) + de (的) + qìhòu (气候 , climate) = Běi jīng de qìhòu (北京的气候 the climate in Beijing)

   cíhuì (词汇 words, vocabulary) + de (的) + mìmì (秘密 secret) = cí huì de mìmì (词汇的秘密 secrets of vocabulary)

3. To build up words referring to specific categories. Example:

   chī (吃 , eat) + de (的) = chī de (吃的 food; things to eat)

   wán (玩 , play) + de (的) = wán de (玩的 toy; something for fun)

   kān mén (看门 , guard the door) + de (的) = kān mén de (看门的 door keeper)

   mù tou (木头 , wood; log) + de (的) = mù tou de (木头的 wooden; made of wood)

Besides, 的 has other two pronunciations corresponding to different meanings. Example:

   mù (目 eye) + dì (的 target) = mù dì (目的 purpose, target)

   biāo (标 target; mark) + dì (的 target) = biāo dì (标的 target)

   dí (的 pure) + què (确 sure; certain) = dí què (的确 indeed; really)

The character 的 also helps to clarify the internal structure of a sentence, marking out the borders between (or among) the words in a sentence. Meanwhile, it also helps to make expressions more succinct. Example:

   Zhèyàng de qíngkuàng shì bù kě jiēshòu de。

   这样的情况是不可接受的。

   The situation like this is totally unacceptable.

   Wǒmen de péngyǒu shì zuótiān dào Běi jīng de。

   我们的朋友是昨天到北京的。

   Our friends arrived Beijing yesterday.

Top 2: 一 (yī)

It frequently happens that the simpler something seems to be, the more comprehensive it actually is. It fits for the character 一. Though it is the simplest character with only one stroke, it has complicated meanings and functions. A lot of words are generated from this one character.

Pay attention to this: In oral language, in order to make the pronunciation sound more natural and easy, people would change its tones, which is largely decided by personal habit.

Core Meanings:

1. one, a, an

2. same

3. whole

4. each, every

考试热词 HOT WORDS FOR TESTS

yì (一 one) + bān (般 , type) = yì bān (一般 ordinary; generally)

yí (一 one) + bèi (辈 generation) + zi (子 , suffix) = yí bèi zi (一辈子 one's whole life)

yì (一 one) + biān (边 side) = yì biān (一边 at the same time; while)

yí (一 one) + dàn (旦 time; day) = yí dàn (一旦 once)

yì (一 one) + diǎn (点 dot; point) + er (儿 suffix) = yì diǎnr (一点儿 a little; a bit)

yí (一 one) + dìng (定 settle; decide) = yí dìng (一定 for sure; must)

yí (一 one) + dù (度 pass; spend) = yí dù (一度 once; for a time)

yí (一 whole) + gòng (共 together; all) = yí gòng (一共 total; altogether)

yí (一 whole) + guàn (贯 pass through) = yí guàn (一贯 all the time; always)

yí (一 one) + huì (会 see; meet) + er (儿 suffix) = yí huìr (一会儿 for a while)

yì (一 one) + liú (流 flow; level) = yì liú (一流 best; first class)

yí (一 whole) + lǜ (律 law; regulation) = yí lǜ (一律 all; without exception)

yí (一 one) + mù (目 eye) + liǎo (了 clear; distinct) + rán (然 so; right) = yí mù liǎo rán (一目了然 be clear at a glance)

yì (一 whole) + qǐ (起 get up; begin) = yì qǐ (一起 together)

yí (一 every) + qiè (切 correspond to; fit to) = yíqiè (一切 every, all)

yí (一 one) + xià (下 classifier for actions) = yí xià (一下 for one time; suddenly)

yí (一 one) + xiàng (向 direction) = yí xiàng (一向 always)

yí (一 same) + yàng (样 type) = yí yàng (一样 same; alike)

yí (一 one) + zài (再 again) = yí zài (一再 always; again and again)

yì (一 same) + zhí (直 direct; straight) = yì zhí (一直 always ; all the time)

yí (一 same) + zhì (致 deliver; send) = yí zhì (一致 accordance; unanimous)

tǒng (统 unite) + yī (一 one) = tǒng yī (统一 unify)

wàn (万 ten thousand) + yī (一 one) = wàn yī (万一 in case)

yì(一 one) + fān (帆 sail) + fēng (风 wind) + shùn (顺 smooth; good) = yì fān fēng shùn (一帆风顺 roses all the way)

yì(一 one) + jǔ (举 do; act) + liǎng (两 two) + dé (得 get; gain) = yì jǔ liǎng dé (一举两得 kill two birds with one stone)

yì(一 one) + rú (如 like) + jì(既 be) + wǎng (往) = yì rú jì wǎng (一如既往 as always)

yì (一 one) + sī (丝 slice) + bù (不 no; not) + gǒu (苟 careless) = yì sī bùgǒu (一丝不苟 dot one's i's and cross one's t's)

Top 3 是 (shì)

Core Meanings:

1. yes; affirmative

2. correct; right

3. this; these

4. be

When building sentences, 是 has almost the same function as the word "be". That's why this character can be in the top ranking of the most frequently used characters. A unique feature is that 是 will never change its appearance, neither with the tenses, nor the changes of plural and singular forms. Example:

Jīntiān shì xīngqīyī。

今天是星期一。

Today is Monday.

Zuótiān shìxīngqīrì。

昨天是星期日。

It was Sunday yesterday.

Tā céngjīng shì wǒde tóngshì。

他曾经是我的同事。

He once had been my colleague.

Tāmen xiànzài shì tóngshì。

他们现在是同事。

They are colleagues now.

考试热词 HOT WORDS FOR TESTS

shì (是 correct) + fēi (非 wrong) = shì fēi (是非 right and wrong; dispute)

shì (是 yes) + fǒu (否 no) = shì fǒu (是否 whether; if)

yào (要 should; would) + shì (是 yes) = yào shì(要是 if; in case)

zǒng (总 always) + shì (是 be) = zǒng shì(总是 always)

fán (凡 all) + shì (是 be) = fán shì(凡是 all; any; every)

kě (可 but) + shì (是 be) = kě shì (可是 but; however)

dàn (但 but) + shì (是 be) = dàn shì(但是 but; however)

yú (于 at; on) + shì (是 be) = yú shì (于是 then; thus)

shí (实 real; concrete) + shì (事 matter; case) + qiú (求 seek; ask for) + shì (是 correct; right) = shí shì qiú shì(实事求是 seek truth from realistic)

Top 4 了 (le)

In sentences, 了 is frequently used to indicate that something happened in a past time, or to say, it helps to indicate the past tense. In this case, 了 should be pronounced with a slight tone "le".

了 can also be used as a suffix to create words. In this case, 了 actually has no physical meaning. Examples:

wéi (为 for; in order to) + le (了) = wèi le (为了 for; in order to)

chú (除 , except; besides) + le (了) = chú le (除了 except; besides)

This character also has other pronunciations and meanings.

Case 1: 了 (liǎo)

Core Meanings:

1. finish; end; terminate

2. understand; recognize; realize

Because 了 has several meanings and pronunciations, it would bring confusion in everyday language. Here is a typical example:

Tā yǐjīng liǎole zhè jiàn shì。

他已经 了了 这件 事。

He has already finished this matter.

The first 了 in the above sentence means "finish" and it should be pronounced as "liǎo". The second is used to indicate the past tense, thus its pronunciation is "le".

Case 2: 了 (liào)

watch; observe

考试热词 HOT WORDS FOR TESTS

liǎo (了 finish) + bù (不 no; not) + qǐ (起 up, rise) = liǎo bù qǐ (了不起 marvelous; amazing)

liǎo (了 understand) + jiě (解 , resolve; decode) = liǎo jiě (了解 know; understand)

bù (不 no; not) + dé (得 , get; auxiliary word) + liǎo (了 finish) = bù dé liǎo (不得了 horrible; Outrageous; awful)

shòu (受 bear; carry) + bú (不 no; not) + liǎo (了 finish) = shòu bù liǎo (受不了 cannot stand sth)

liǎo (了 finish) + duàn (断 , cut) = liǎo duàn (了断 finish; terminate)

liǎo (了 finish) + jié (结 , end) = liǎo jié (了结 end; finish)

liǎo (了 finish) + què (却 stop) = liǎo què (了却 settle, solve)

miǎn (免 exempt; dismiss) + bú (不 no; not) + liǎo (了 finish) = miǎn bù liǎo (免不了 be unavoidable)

shǎo (少 less; reduce) + bú (不 no; not) + liǎo (了 finish) = shǎo bù liǎo (少不了 cannot dispense with)

liǎo (了 understand) + rú (如 like) + zhǐ (指 finger) + zhǎng (掌 palm) = liǎo rú zhǐ zhǎng (了如指掌 at one's fingertips)

Top 5 我 (wǒ)

One thing for sure is that, in every language in the world, the words referring to "I" are always on the top rankings of the most frequently used words. It is quite interesting that, in Chinese, wǒ (我) has rather extensive meanings:

1. I; me

2. Our party, our side

考试热词 HOT WORDS FOR TESTS

wàng (忘 forget) + wǒ (我 I; me) = wàng wǒ (忘我 selfless)

zì (自 self) + wǒ (我 I; me) = zì wǒ (自我 oneself; ego)

wéi (唯 only) + wǒ (我 I; me) + dú (独 alone) + zūn (尊 respect; outstanding) = wéi wǒ dú zūn (唯我独尊 egoistic; everything but mine)

ěr (尔 you) + yú (虞 cheat) + wǒ (我 I; me) + zhà (诈 cheat) = ěr yú wǒ zhà (尔虞我诈 deceive and blackmail each other) shí (时 time) + bú (不 no; not) + wǒ (我 I; me) + dài (待 wait) = shí bù wǒ dài (时不我待 Time waits for no man)

wǒ (我 I; me) + xíng (行 act; behave) + wǒ (我 I; me) + sù (素 as usual; always) = wǒ xíng wǒ sù (我行我素 persist one's old ways)

002

Immortal Bricks

Chinese Characters

Many learners have experienced this form of teaching: While the teacher is trying to explain some basic knowledge about Chinese characters, he or she would show how Chinese people create the character 日 (rì, sun; day) like creating a sketch painting for the sun. Indeed, that is one of the ways to create Chinese characters and actually, there are only a few parts of the characters that were created in this way.

Even today, people cannot figure out the exact time of the birth of Chinese characters. Generally speaking, those ancient characters appeared on the animal bones that were dated about 5,000 years ago, and are regarded as the primary ancestors for modern characters. Their appearances have changed a lot over the years and only a few people in current times can recognize them.

One amazing fact is that many characters that were created thousands years ago are still in use even though they have changed a lot in their appearance. People can find a distinct route of their evolution. The chart below shows the typical changes of the appearances during the past thousands of years. Nowadays, the simplified Chinese characters are popularly used in mainland China, while the traditional ones are still in use in Hong Kong, Taiwan, and many China towns all over the world.

To some extent, the Chinese characters break the limitations of time and space. Because the continuous existence of the characters, people in modern times can know more about the history of the past. Today, people still cannot understand each other well in oral language due to the influences of the dialects, but people can understand each other well in the written language.

For many learners, it really is a huge difficulty to memorize

These pictographic characters carved in an ox scapula are from more than 3500 years ago and are called oracle-bone inscriptions. They are considered the rudiment of modern day characters. The content of this one means: one country attacked another twice and obtained 31 war prisoners.

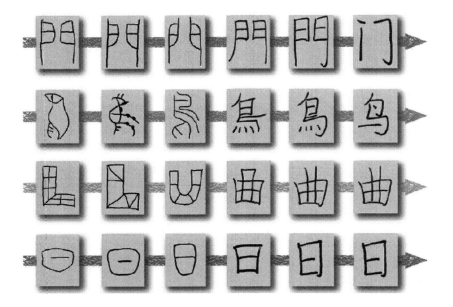

thousands of Chinese characters. Some of my friends even complained that the Mandarin Chinese and English seemed to be from two different planets. They are right to some extent: English and Chinese belong to two totally different language systems: English is typically a Phonetic Language (Biǎo yīn yǔ yán 表音语言), and it uses 26 letters to record the sounds of words, while Chinese is an typical Ideographic Language (biǎo yì yǔ yán 表意语言), and it uses strokes to create numerous symbols (Chinese characters) to record the meanings of words.

One frustrating reality is that learners cannot get any hint for the pronunciation from the appearance of a character. There is no shortcut for this and you have to make the effort to memorize the strokes and pronunciations of the different characters. Even native Chinese speakers have to do that. Many Chinese teachers found their students to have great talent on their calligraphy lectures with Chinese brush pen, and many times the works by beginners brought a big surprise to the people.

By the way, I do find that many learners prefer to using Pinyin in their study and would not like to make efforts in grasping Chinese characters. It is sure that Pinyin will bring them an easy start, but one can never really grasp this language without knowing characters. A good news is that, with only 800 frequently used characters, you can almost handle the everyday language, and if you can learn 2,500 characters, you are invincible!

WORDS BANK

Frequently Used Pictographic Characters

The following characters are generated by the "painting" technique, but people cannot find any traces of the original objects from their modern day appearances.

日 (rì)

sun; day

考试热词 HOT WORDS FOR TESTS

rì (日 day) + cháng (常 , usual) = rìcháng (日常 every day; usual)

rì (日 day) + chéng (程 procedure; route) = rì chéng (日程 schedule)

rì (日 day) + jì (记 record) = rì jì (日记 dairy; log)

rì (日 day) + lì (历 experience) = rì lì (日历 calendar)

rì (日 day) + qī (期 period) = rì qī (日期 day; date)

rì (日 day) + xīn (新 new) + yuè (月 month) + yì (异 different) = rì xīn yuè yì (日新月异 change quickly)

rì (日 day) + yì (益 more) = rì yì (日益 day by day; increasingly)

rì (日 day) + yòng (用 use) + pǐn (品 item; article) = rì yòng pǐn (日用品 daily necessities)

rì (日 day) + zǐ (子 suffix) = rì zi (日子 day; time)

月 (yuè)

moon; month

考试热词 HOT WORDS FOR TESTS

suì (岁 year) + yuè (月 month) = suì yuè (岁月 time)

yuè (月 moon) + liàng (亮 light) = yuè liang (月亮 moon)

zhēng (正 first) + yuè (月 month) = zhēng yuè (正月 first month in Chinese lunar calendar)

yuè (月 month) + bǐng (饼 cake) = yuè bǐng (月饼 moon cake)

yuè (月 month) + jīng (经 menses) = yuè jīng (月经 menses)

yuè (月 moon) + qiú (球 ball) = yuè qiú (月球 moon)

là (腊 sacrifices to the gods) + yuè (月 moon) = là yuè (the twelfth month in Chinese lunar calendar)

mì (蜜 honey) + yuè (月 month) = mì yuè (蜜月 honeymoon)

nián (年 year) + yuè (月 month) = nián yuè (年月 time)

cháng (长 long) + nián (年 year) + lěi (累 repeated) + yuè (月 month) = cháng nián lěi yuè (长年累月 over the years)

fēng (风 wind) + huā (花 flower) + xuě (雪 snow) + yuè (月 moon) = fēng huā xuě yuè (风花雪月 romantic themes)

hóu (猴 monkey) + nián (年 year) + mǎ (马 horse) + yuè (月 month) = hóu nián mǎ yuè (猴年马月 till the cows come home; few and far between)

人 (rén)

human; people

考试热词 HOT WORDS FOR TESTS

sī (私 private) + rén (人 people) = sī rén (私人)

xíng (行 walk) + rén (人 people) = xíng rén (行人 pedestrian)

zhǔ (主 major) + rén (人 people) = zhǔ rén (主人 owner; master)

běn (本 root; this) + rén (人 people) = běn rén (本人 oneself; I; me)

bié (别 other) + rén (人 people) = bié rén (别人 other people)

chéng (成 mature) + rén (人 people) = chéng rén (成人 adult)

dí (敌 hostile) + rén (人 people) = dí rén (敌人 enemy)

diū (丢 lost) + rén (人 people) = diū rén (丢人 be disgraced)

fǎ (法 law) + rén (人 people) = fǎ rén (法人 legal person)

fū (夫 husband) + rén (人 people) = fū rén (夫人 wife)

gè (个 individual) + rén (人 people) = gè rén (个人 personal)

gōng (工 work) + rén (人 people) = gōng rén (工人 worker)

kè (客 guest) + rén (人 people) = kè rén (客人 guest)

mí (迷 enthusiast) + rén (人 people) = mí rén (迷人 charming)

rén (人 people) + cái (才 talent) = rén cái (人才 person with excellent ability; talents)

rén (人 people) + dào (道 way; reason) = rén dào (人道 humanity)

rén (人 people) + gé (格 character) = rén gé (人格 personality)

rén (人 people) + gōng (工 work) = rén gōng (人工 man-made; artificial)

rén (人 people) + jiā (家 home) = rén jiā (人家 household;)
rén (人 people) + jia (家 home) = rén jia (人家 other; another)
rén (人 people) + jiān (间 space) = rén jiān (人间 the world)
rén (人 people) + kǒu (口 mouth) = rén kǒu (人口 population)
rén (人 people) + lèi (类 kind) = rén lèi (人类 mankind)
rén (人 people) + shēng (生 life) = rén shēng (人生 life)
rén (人 people) + shì (士 scholar) = rén shì (人士 personage; public figure)
rén (人 people) + shì (事 matter) = rén shì (人事 human affairs; personal matters)
rén (人 people) + wéi (为 do; behave) = rén wéi (人为 man-made; factitious)
rén (人 people) + wù (物 object) = rén wù (人物 character; personage)
rén (人 people) + xìng (性 nature; property) = rén xìng (人性 humanity; human nature)
rén (人 people) + yuán (员 individual) = rén yuán (人员 staff; individual)
rén (人 people) + zhì (质 pledge) = rén zhì (人质 hostage)
dāng (当 at; on) + shì (事 matter) + rén (人 people) = dāng shì rén (当事人 party; client)
rén (人 people) + mín (民 people) + bì (币 currency) = rén mín bì (人民币 Chinese Yen; RMB)
fēng (风 tradition) + tǔ (土 land) + rén (人 people) + qíng (情 situation) = fēng tǔ rén qíng (风土人情 local conditions and customs)

口 (kǒu)

mouth; gate

考试热词 HOT WORDS FOR TESTS

chū (出 get out) + kǒu (口 gate) = chū kǒu (出口 exit; export)
gǎng (港 port) + kǒu (口 gate) = gáng kǒu (港口 port)
jiè (借 borrow) + kǒu (口 mouth) = jiè kǒu (借口 excuse)
jìn (进 enter) + kǒu (口 gate) = jìn kǒu (进口 entrance; import)
kě (可 good) + kǒu (口 mouth) = ké kǒu (可口 delicious)
kǒu (口 mouth) + qì (气 gas; atmosphere) = kǒu qì (口气 smell of mouth; tone)
kǒu (口 mouth) + qiāng (腔 cavity; hole) = kǒu qiāng (口腔 mouth; oral cavity)
kǒu (口 mouth) + tóu (头 top) = kǒu tóu (口头 verbal)
kǒu (口 mouth) + wèi (味 taste) = kǒu wèi (口味 taste; flavor)

kǒu (口 mouth) + yīn (音 sound) = kǒu yīn (口音 accent)
quē (缺 lost; lack) + kǒu (口 gate) = quē kǒu (缺口 gap; insufficiency)
rù (入 enter) + kǒu (口 gate) = rù kǒu (入口 entrance)
wèi (胃 stomach) + kǒu (口 mouth) = wèi kǒu (胃口 apatite)

手 (shǒu)

hand; person (doing a certain job)

考试热词 HOT WORDS FOR TESTS

shǒu (手 hand) + biǎo (表 clock) = shóu biǎo (手表 watch)
shǒu (手 hand) + fǎ (法 method) = shóu fǎ (手法 way; skill)
shǒu (手 hand) + gōng (工 work) = shǒu gōng (手工 handcraft)
shǒu (手 hand) + jī (机 machine; mobile) = shǒu jī (手机 mobile phone)
shǒu (手 hand) + shì (势 trend; situation) = shǒu shì (手势 gesture)
shǒu (手 hand) + shù (术 way; skill) = shǒu shù (手术 operation)
shǒu (手 hand) + tào (套 cover; knot) = shǒu tào (手套 gloves)
shǒu (手 hand) + xù (续 continue) = shǒu xù (手续 formality; procedure)
shǒu (手 hand) + yì (艺 art) = shǒu yì (手艺 skill; craftsmanship)
shǒu (手 hand) + zhǐ (指 finger) = shóu zhǐ (手指 finger)
suí (随 with) + shǒu (手 hand) = suí shǒu (随手 carelessly)
wò (握 grasp) + shǒu (手 hand) = wò shǒu (握手 shake hand)
xǐ (洗 wash) + shǒu (手 hand) = xíshǒu (洗手 wash hand)
xí shǒu (洗手 wash hand) + jiān (间 space; room) = xí shǒu jiān (洗手间 bathroom)
xiōng (凶 fierce) + shǒu (手 person) = xiōng shǒu (凶手 murder)
xuǎn (选 select) + shǒu (手 person) = xuǎn shǒu (选手 candidate)
zhù (助 help) + shǒu (手 person) = zhù shǒu (助手 assistant)
zhuó (着 consign; launch) + shǒu (手 hand) = zhuó shǒu (着手 start working on)
bǎ (把 hold) + shǒu (手 hand) = bǎ shǒu (把手 handle)
dòng (动 move; start) + shǒu (手 hand) = dòng shǒu (动手 start work; fight)
duì (对 opposite) + shǒu (手 person) = duì shǒu (对手 opponent)

fēn (分 separate; depart) + shǒu (手 hand) = fēn shǒu (分手 separate; break up)

ná (拿 take; hold) + shǒu (手 hand) = ná shǒu (拿手 be good at)

bú (不 no; not) + zé (择 chose) + shǒu (手 hand) + duàn (段 section; stage) = bù zé shǒu duàn (不择手段 By fair means or foul)

ài (爱 love) + bú (不 no; not) + shì (释 release) + shǒu (手 hand) = ài bú shì shǒu (爱不释手 fondle admiringly)

山 (shān)

mountain; hill

考试热词 HOT WORDS FOR TESTS

pá (爬 climb) + shān (山 mountain) = pá shān (爬山 climb the mountain)

shān (山 mountain) + mài (脉 pulse) = shān mài (山脉 mountain chain)

shān (山 mountain) + chuān (川 mountain) = shān chuān (山川 mountains)

shān (山 mountain) + fēng (峰 summit) = shān fēng (山峰 summit; peak)

shān (山 mountain) + gǔ (谷 valley) = shān gǔ (山谷 valley)

shān (山 mountain) + yá (崖 cliff) = shān yá (山崖 cliff)

shān (山 mountain) + yáng (羊 sheep; goat) = shān yáng (山羊 goat)

huǒ (火 fire) + shān (山 mountain) = huǒ shān (火山 volcano)

dēng (登 climb) + shān (山 mountain) = dēng shān (登山 mountaineering)

kào (靠 lean; rely) + shān (山 mountain) = kào shān (靠山 backer; patron)

xuě (雪 snow) + shān (山 mountain) = xuě shān (雪山 snow mountain)

水 (shuǐ)

water; river; flood

考试热词 HOT WORDS FOR TESTS

xīn (薪 salary; firewood) + shuǐ (水 water) = xīn shuǐ (薪水 salary)

dàn (淡 thin; tasteless) + shuǐ (水 water) = dàn shuǐ (淡水 fresh water)

hóng (洪 flood) + shuǐ (水 water) = hóng shuǐ (洪水 flood)

jiāo (胶 glue) + shuǐ (水 water) = jiāo shuǐ (胶水 glue)

kāi (开 boiled; open) + shuǐ (水 water) = kāi shuǐ (开水 boiled water)

kuàng (矿 mineral) + quán (泉 spring) + shuǐ (水 water) = kuàng quán shuǐ (矿泉水 mineral water)
mò (墨 black; ink) + shuǐ (水 water) + ér (儿 suffix) = mò shuǐr (墨水儿 ink)
qián (潜 dive) + shuǐ (水 water) = qián shuǐ (潜水 dive)
shuǐ (水 water) + guǒ (果 fruit) = shuí guǒ (水果 fruit)
shuǐ (水 water) + lì (利 benefit; facility) = shuǐ lì (水利 water conservancy)
shuǐ (水 water) + lóng (龙 dragon) + tóu (头 head) = shuǐ lóng tóu (水龙头 faucet; tap)
shuǐ (水 water) + ní (泥 mud) = shuǐ ní (水泥 cement; concrete)
shuǐ (水 water) + píng (平 horizontal) = shuǐ píng (水平 level)

003

Origin of the Legend

Characters and Words

For most of the languages, the "words" are the most basic elements that are used to construct whole language systems, and the words "mirror" all of the objects or concepts in our lives.

In theory, an independent word is constructed with three essential elements:

a) A fixed basic appearance;

b) One fixed pronunciation (or more);

c) One concrete meaning or function (or more).

In comparison to the above three elements, in most cases, a single character equals one word. What's more, it is quite common that a character have several different meanings. For example:

信 (xìn)

Meaning 1: letter

xìn (信 letter) + fēng (封 seal) = xìn fēng (信封 envelop)

xìn (信 letter) + jiàn (件 piece) = xìn jiàn (信件 letter)

Meaning 2: message; signal

xìn (信 signal) + hào (号 mark) = xìn hào(信号 signal)

xìn(信 message) + xī(息 news) = xìn xī (信息 information)

Meaning 3: trust; belief

xìn (信 trust) + lài (赖 lean on) = xìn lài (信赖 trust; rely on)

xìn (信 belief) + niàn (念 think; miss) = xìn niàn (信念 faith; belief)

Meaning 4: reputation; credibility

xìn (信 credibility) + yòng(用 use) = xìn yòng(信用 credibility)

xìn yòng(信用 credibility) + kǎ (卡 card) = xìn yòng kǎ (信用卡 credit card)

In the Chinese language, there indeed some characters that don't fit the standards to be the "words". Here is an example:

槟榔 (bīn láng)

areca-nut

Of course, 槟 (bīn) has its pronunciation and appearance, but it has no concrete and independent meaning, neither does the character 榔 (láng). So, neither of these two characters can be regarded as "words". Only the combination "槟榔" functions as an independent word.

Here is another example: 蝴 (hú) is not a "word" due to the lack of concrete meaning by itself, and it always go with 蝶 (dié) to make a word as 蝴蝶 (hú dié, butterfly). Meanwhile, 蝶 is regarded as a "word" for it has the meaning as "butterfly; sphenoid".

It frequently happens in the Chinese language that a character, or to say, a word built by one character, will have two or more pronunciations. Such type of characters are called duō yīn zì (多音字, polyphonic character). For example:

背

Case 1: bēi - carry on the back

bēi(背 carry) + fù (负 carry) = bēi fù (背负 carry)

Case 2: bèi - back (body)

bèi (背 back) + jǐng (景 scenery) = bèi jǐng (背 景 background)

Case 3: bèi - betray

bèi (背 betray) + pàn (叛 betray) = bèi pàn (背 叛 betray)

Case 4: bèi - recite

bèi (背 recite) + sòng(诵 chant) = bèi sòng(背 诵 recite)

In reality, a possible problem in language is that, in some cases, you have to figure out which one of the meanings of a polyphonic character is used. For example:

Case 1:

Tā bēi zhe tā de nǚpéngyou qù le yīyuàn。

他背着他的女朋友去了医院。

He carried his girlfriend with his back.

Case 2:

Tā bèi zhe tā de nǚpéngyou qù le yīyuàn。

他背着他的女朋友去了医院。

He went to the hospital without letting his girlfriend know.

Though the above sentences in Chinese seem completely the same in appearance, the meanings of 背 brings totally different meanings.

In Mandarin Chinese, there are hundreds of polyphonic characters, and a few of them even have three or more pronunciations. You might have a question like this: Why did Chinese people create so many characters like that, in spite of the difficulties in understanding and using? A possible answer could be: As time goes by, people need more and more basic words, but they would not like to use more and more characters in everyday language because it would also increase the difficulty in application. Then a compromising way is to merge more meanings along with pronunciations into one character.

Indeed, for most beginners, it is quite difficult to grasp the polyphonic characters. A suggestion is that you accumulate the knowledge little by little. You will also find that, with the help of context, it is not that difficult to determine the correct meaning and pronunciation.

WORDS BANK

The following list shows some polyphonic characters and words created by them, which frequently appear in language tests.

便

Case 1: biàn

convenient; convenience

HOT WORDS FOR TESTS

biàn (便 convenient) + lì (利 convenient) = biàn lì (便利 convenient)

biàn (便 convenient) + tiáo (条 note) = biàn tiáo (便条 tip)

biàn (便 convenient) + yú (于 at; on) = biàn yú (便于 easy to; convenient for)

fāng (方 just; side) + biàn (便 convenient) = fāng biàn (方便 convenient)

shùn (顺 follow; along) + biàn (便 convenient) = shùn biàn (顺便 by the way)

yǐ (以 for; by) + biàn (便 convenient) = yǐ biàn (以便 so that; in order to)

suí (随 follow; along) + biàn (便 convenient) = suí biàn (随便 random; informal)

Case 2: biàn

then; thus

Example:

jí (即 as; since) + biàn (便 then; thus) = jí biàn (既便 even; even if)

Case 3: pián

cheap; affordable

Example:

pián (便 cheap) + yí (宜 good; fit) = pián yi (便宜 cheap; affordable)

和

Case 1: hé

1. and

2. peace; peaceful; harmony

3. unite; integrate

考试热词 HOT WORDS FOR TESTS

nǐ (你 you) + hé (和 and) + wǒ (我 I; me) = nǐ hé wǒ (你和我 you and me)

hé (和 peaceful) + ǎi (蔼 grace; graceful) = hé ǎi (和蔼 kind; graceful)

hé (和 peace) + jiě (解 settle) = hé jiě (和解 compromise; reconciliation)

hé (和 harmony) + mù (睦 harmony) = hé mù (和睦 harmony; harmonious)

hé (和 peace) + píng (平 calm) = hé píng (和平 peace; peaceful)

hé (和 peaceful) + qì (气 air; atmosphere) = hé qì (和气 kind; harmonious)

hé (和 harmony) + xié (谐 harmonic) = hé xié (和谐 harmony; harmonious)

huǎn (缓 ease; relax) + hé (和 peace) = huǎn hé (缓和 relax; mitigate)

róu (柔 gentle; soft) + hé (和 peace) = róu hé (柔和 gentle; mild)

tiáo (调 adjust) + hé (和 harmonious) = tiáo hé (调和 reconcile; compromise)

wēn (温 tender) + hé (和 peaceful) = wēn hé (温和 gentle; mild)

gòng (共 together; all) + hé (和 unite) + guó (国 nation) = gòng hé guó (共和国 republic)

Case 2: hè

follow; response; echo

Example:

fù (附 attach; adhere) + hè (和 echo) = fù hè (附和 chime in with; echo)

yī (一 one) + chàng (唱 sing) + yī (一 one) + hè (和 echo) = yí chàng yī hè (一唱一和 echo each other)

Case 3: huó

warm

Example:

nuǎn (暖 warm) + hé (和 warm) = nuǎn huo (暖和 warm)

Case 4: hú

complete (a set in mahjong)

hú (和 complete) + pái (牌 mahjong; board) = hú pái (和牌 complete a set in mahjong)

干

case1: gān

1. dry
2. complete; finish
3. disturb
4. related; relative

考试热词 HOT WORDS FOR TESTS

gān (干 finish) + bēi (杯 glass; cup) = gān bēi (干杯 cheers; bottoms up)
gān (干 dry) + cuì (脆 crisp) = gān cuì (干脆 dry and crisp; straightforward)
gān (干 dry) + hàn (旱 drought) = gān hàn (干旱 drought)
gān (干 dry) + zào (燥 dry; arid) = gān zào (干燥 dry; arid)
gān (干 dry) + jìng (净 clean) = gān jìng (干净 clean)
bǐng (饼 cake; pastry) + gān (干 dry) = bǐng gān (饼干 biscuit; cookie)
gān (干 disturb) + rǎo (扰 disturb) = gān rǎo (干扰 disturb)
gān (干 disturb) + shè (涉 engage) = gān shè (干涉 intervene; interference)
gān (干 disturb) + yù (预 engage) = gān yù (干预 intervene; interpose)
ruò (若 like; seem) + gān (干 related) = ruò gān (若干 some; a number of)

Case 2: gàn

1. do; work
2. talent; expertise
3. backbone; key

考试热词 HOT WORDS FOR TESTS

gàn (干 do) + huó (活 job) + ér (儿 suffix) = gàn huór (干活 work; do one's job)
néng (能 can; capability) + gàn (干 do) = néng gàn (能干 capable)
gàn (干 do) + jìn (劲 strength) = gàn jìn (干劲 vigor; enthusiasm)
cái (才 talent) + gàn (干 talent) = cái gàn (才干 talent; expertise)
gǔ (骨 bone) + gàn (干 backbone) = gǔ gàn (骨干 backbone; key staff)

重

Case 1: zhòng

1. heavy; weight
2. emphasize; important
3. serious

考试热词 HOT WORDS FOR TESTS

zhòng (重 heavy) + liàng (量 quantity) = zhòng liàng (重量 weight)

bǐ (比 ratio; compare) + zhòng (重 weight) = bǐ zhòng (比重 proportion)

chén (沉 heavy) + zhòng (重 heavy) = chén zhòng (沉重 heavy)

zhòng (重 weight) + xīn (心 heart) = zhòng xīn (重心 center of gravity)

zhòng (重 important) + ciǎn (点 dot; point) = zhòng diǎn (重点 key point)

zhòng (重 important) + cà (大 big; huge) = zhòng dà (重大 great; significant)

rèn (任 duty) + zhòng (重 heavy) + dào (道 road; way) + yuǎn (远 far) = rèn zhòng dào yuǎn (任重道远 long way to go)

jǔ (举 move; rise) + zú (足 foot) + qīng (轻 light) + zhòng (重 heavy) = jǔ zú qīng zhòng (举足轻重 decisive; hold the balance)

lóng (隆 grand) + zhòng (重 serious) = lóng zhòng (隆重 solemn; ceremonious)

shèn (慎 cautious) + zhòng (重 serious) = shèn zhòng (慎重 careful; cautious)

yán (严 sever; serious) + zhòng (重 serious) = yán zhòng (严重 serious)

zhèng (郑 formally) + zhòng (重 serious) = zhèng zhòng (郑重 solemn; earnest)

zhuāng (庄 solemn) + zhòng (重 serious) = zhuāng zhòng (庄重 solemn; earnest)

zhòng (重 important) + shì (视 view; see) = zhòng shì (重视 attach importance to)

zhòng (重 important) + yào (要 key; important) = zhòng yào (重要 important)

zhù (注 input; focus) + zhòng (重 important) = zhù zhòng (注重 pay attention to; lay emphasis on)

zhuó (着 assign) + zhòng (重 important) = zhuó zhòng (着重 lay emphasis on)

zūn (尊 respect) + zhòng (重 important) = zūn zhòng (尊重 respect)

bǎo (保 keep; guard) + zhòng (重 important) = bǎo zhòng (保重 take care)

Case 2: chóng

repeat; again; duplicate

22

考试热词 HOT WORDS FOR TESTS

chóng (重 duplicate) + dié (叠 fold) = chóng dié (重叠 overlap)

chóng (重 repeat) + fù (复 again) = chóng fù (重复 repeat)

chóng (重 repeat) + xīn (新 new) = chóng xīn (重新 anew; again)

结

Case 1: jié

1. connect; tie; knot

2. end; conclusion; finish; complete

考试热词 HOT WORDS FOR TESTS

jié (结 knot) + gòu (构 structure) = jié gòu (结构 structure)

jié (结 connect) + hé (合 join; joint) = jié hé (结合 join; integrate)

jié (结 knot) + jīng (晶 crystal) = jié jīng (结晶 crystal; crystallize)

jié (结 end) + jú (局 case; situation) = jié jú (结局 end; result)

jié (结 end) + lùn (论 argue; discuss) = jié lùn (结论 conclusion)

jié (结 end) + shù (束 bound; tie) = jié shù (结束 end; finish)

jié (结 end) + suàn (算 calculate) = jié suàn (结算 settle accounts)

jié (结 finish) + zhàng (账 debt) = jié zhàng (结账 check out)

tuán (团 unite) + jié (结 knot) = tuán jié (团结 unite)

zǒng (总 general; all) + jié (结 conclude) = zǒng jié (总结 summary; conclusion)

bā (巴 cling to; wish) + jié (结 tie) = bā jie (巴结 fawn on; carry favor with)

dòng (冻 freeze) + jié (结 finish) = dòng jié (冻结 frost; frozen account)

gōu (勾 induce; draw) + jié (结 connect) = gōu jié (勾结 collude with; gang up with)

jié (结 tie) + hūn (婚 marriage) = jié hūn (结婚 marriage)

Case 2: jiē

1. produce; grow

2. stammer; solid

考试热词 HOT WORDS FOR TESTS

jiē (结 grow) + guǒ (果 fruit; result) = jiēguǒ (结果 result; consequence; produce fruits)

jiē (结 solid) + shí (实 solid) = jiē shi (结实 solid)

数

Case 1: shù

number; digit

考试热词 HOT WORDS FOR TESTS

shù (数 number) + é (额 sum; quantity) = shù é (数额 quantity)

shù (数 digit) + jù (据 evidence) = shù jù (数据 data)

shù (数 number) + liàng (量 quantity) = shù liàng (数量 quantity)

shù (数 digit) + mǎ (码 code) = shù mǎ (数码 digital)

shù (数 number) + xué (学 subject; discipline) = shù xué (数学 math)

shù (数 number) + zì (字 letter) = shù zì (数字 number; digit)

suàn (算 calculate) + shù (数 number) = suàn shù (算数 calculate; math)

wú (无 no; not) + shù (数 number) = wú shù (无数 countless; innumerable)

Case: shǔ

1. count; calculate

2. blame

考试热词 HOT WORDS FOR TESTS

shǔ (数 count) + bú (不 no; not) + 胜 (bear; carry) + shǔ (数 count) = shǔ bú shèng shǔ (数不胜数 countless; beyond count)

shǔ (数 count) + 一 (yī one) + shǔ (数 count) + èr (二 two) = shǔ yi shǔ èr (数一数二 one of the best)

shǔ (数 blame) + luò (落 down) = shǔ luò (数落 blame; scold)

调

Case 1: tiáo

1. adjust; shift

2. modify; modulate

3. tease, make fun of

考试热词 HOT WORDS FOR TESTS

tiáo (调 adjust) + jì (剂 doze) = tiáo jì (调剂 adjust; regulate)

tiáo (调 adjust) + jié (节 knob; section) = tiáo jié (调节 adjust; modify)

tiáo (调 modulate) + jiě (解 settle; solve) = tiáo jiě (调解 mediate; reconcile)

tiáo (调 adjust) + liào (料 material) = tiáo liào (调料 flavor; seasoning)

tiáo (调 modify) + zhěng (整 pack) = tiáo zhěng (调整 adjust; modulate)

xié (协 coordinate) + tiáo (调 modify) = xié tiáo (协调 coordinate; harmonize)

kōng (空 air) + tiáo (调 adjust) = kōng tiáo (空调 air conditioner)

tiáo (调 tease) + pí (皮 naughty) = tiáo pí (调皮 naughty; piquant; rascal)

tiáo (调 tease) + xì (戏 tease; play with) = tiáo xì (调戏 molest)

Case 2: diào

1. tone; melody

2. invest; survey

3. mobilize; assign

考试热词 HOT WORDS FOR TESTS

dān (单 single) + diào (调 tone) = dān diào (单调 monotonous; dull)

shēng (声 voice) + diào (调 tone) = shēng diào (声调)

qiáng (强 strong; strengthen) + diào (调 tone) = qiáng diào (强调 emphasize)

diào (调 invest) + chá (查 check; examine) = diào chá (调查 investigate)

diào (调 mobilize) + dòng (动 move) = diào dòng (调动 transfer; remove)

长

Case 1: cháng

1. long; extended; length

2. be good at; expertise

考试热词 HOT WORDS FOR TESTS

cháng (长 long) + chéng (城 city; castle) = cháng chéng (长城 the Great Wall)
cháng (长 long) + jiāng (江 river) = cháng jiāng (长江 the Yangtze River)
màn (漫 long) + cháng (长 long) = màn cháng (漫长 endless; far-flung)
cháng (长 long) + tú (途 road; way) = cháng tú (长途 long distance)
yán (延 extend) + cháng (长 long) = yán cháng (延长 extend)
zhuān (专 specialized) + cháng (长 expertise) = zhuān cháng (专长 specialty)
shàn (擅 be good at) + cháng (长 be good at) = shàn cháng (擅长 be skilled in; be adept at)
tè (特 specialty) + cháng (长 expertise) = tè cháng (特长 specialty)

Case 2: zhǎng

1. seniors; leader

2. grow; produce

考试热词 HOT WORDS FOR TESTS

dǒng shì (董事 director) + zhǎng (长 leader) = dǒng shì zhǎng (董事长 chairman; president)
xiào (校 school; college) + zhǎng (长 leader) = xiào zhǎng (校长 principal; school master)
zhǎng (长 senior) + bèi (辈 generation) = zhǎng bèi (长辈 elders; seniority)
chéng (成 become; grow) + zhǎng (长 grow) = chéng zhǎng (成长 grow up)
shēng (生 born) + zhǎng (长 grow) = shēng zhǎng (生长 grow; germinate)
bá (拔 draw) + miáo (苗 sprout; young plant) + zhù (助 help) + zhǎng (长 grow) = bá miáo zhù zhǎng (拔苗助长 spoil things by excessive enthusiasm)

004

Infinite Possibilities

Features of Vocabulary System

If you happen to have both an English dictionary and a Chinese dictionary, compare them and you will find some interesting differences in them. In the English dictionary, each of the words appear as an independent term and is listed in a linear way. In a Chinese dictionary, a character is listed as a major term and followed by sub-terms that are generated from that character. It actually tells you the way the Chinese language built its vocabulary system: By combining two (or more) characters, it can generate numerous words.

This way actually shows the magical power of math. Think about this example: Suppose we have 12 pens with different colors, and if we pick up two from them thus to make a color combination, how many results can we have? The answer is 66! We know that there about 800 characters that are mostly used in everyday language, so if we select two different characters to "create" a word, in theory, we can get 320,400 new words! We don't necessarily need that many words in our everyday language, but what it really matters is that this method brings a huge space for possibilities.

One of the obvious benefits is that people can create words in a more "economic" way. For example: Suppose that we need 100,000 words for describing 100,000 items. In English, people would create 100,000 independent words which are completely different to each other in their appearances. While in Chinese, people would use 800 characters to make combinations to create the words needed. It is more interesting that, suppose people need another more 100, 000 words one hundred years later, in English, people should create another 100,000 words with unique appearances while in Chinese, people can still make use of those 800 characters. So, in the Chinese way, people don't need to create more characters nor need to recognize more.

27

Though this tree growing in the stone wall seems weak, its strength of will and survival really surprises the tourists passing by.

Another benefit is that the characters that are combined for building up a "new" word can give hint to the meanings of the new one. For example, if you know the meanings of 潜 (qián, dive) and 艇 (tǐng, boat; ship), you can easily figure out the meaning of the word 潜艇 (qián tǐng, submarine). Actually, this situation is very popular in Chinese language and it has largely reduced the difficulty of memorizing the meanings of words. More examples:

fēi (飞 fly) + tǐng (艇 boat; ship) = fēi tǐng (飞 艇 airship)

jiù (救 save) + shēng (生 life; live) + tǐng (艇 boat; ship) = jiù shēng tǐng (救生艇 lifeboat)

I am not saying that this way of creating words in Chinese language is better than the ways adopted by other languages. The fact is that each language in the world will find its own best way based on its unique circumstance, just like what happens in the nature: Each creature has build up its own unique surviving way during long period of natural selection.

We know that in most cases, a single character equals to a word, and in some Chinese grammar books, such type of words are defined as 单字词 (dān zì cí), which means "a word formed by one character". But, I personally think that this term is a little bit superficial and does not indicate the true power of these words. They are just like the things listed in a periodic table of elements in our chemical lectures. They can generate numerous things in magical ways. So, in our following discussion, we will use a more pertinent term for them of 源词 (Yuán cí, Origin Word), which refers specifically to a word that is built up only by one character.

WORDS BANK

When you open a Chinese dictionary, you will find that most of the 源词 (yuán cí, Origin Word) have several independent meanings. A few of them are even like a super word, which can combine with many other element words and then generate many "new" words. The following are some super element words that frequently appear in the language exams.

地 dì

1. land; ground; site
2. situation; position
3. functions auxiliary word

考试热词 HOT WORDS FOR TESTS

dì (地 land) + dào (道 road; way) = dì dào (地道 tunnel)

dì (地 land) + dao (道 way; method) = dì dao (地道 authentic; simon-pure)

dì (地 land) + diǎn (点 spot) = dì diǎn (地点 site; location)

dì (地 land) + fāng (方 direction; site) = dì fang (地方 position, site)

dì (地 land) + lǐ (理 reason; theory) = dì lǐ (地理 geography)

dì (地 land) + qiú (球 ball) = dì qiú (地球 earth)

dì (地 site) + qū (区 region) = dì qū (地区 region)

dì (地 land) + shì (势 trend; situation) = dì shì (地势 terrain; topography)

dì (地 land) + tǎn (毯 blanket) = dì tǎn (地毯 carpet; rug)

dì (地 land) + tiě (铁 steel) = dì tiě (地铁 subway; metro)

dì (地 land) + tú (图 picture) = dì tú (地图 map)

dì (地 position) + wèi (位 stage; position) = dì wèi (地位 position; rank)

dì (地 land) + zhèn (震 shake; shock; shake) = dì zhèn (地震 earthquake)

dì (地 site) + zhǐ (址 address; location) = dì zhǐ (地址 address)

dì (地 land) + zhì (质 quality; property) = dì zhì (地质 geology)

lù (陆 land; continent) + dì (地 land) = lù dì (陆地 land)

pén (盆 basin; pot) + dì (地 land) = pén dì (盆地 basin)

tǔ (土 soil) + dì (地 land) = tǔ dì (土地 land; earth)

zhèn (阵 battle array) + dì (地 site) = zhèn dì (阵地 front; position)

zhí mín (殖民 colonize) + dì (地 land) = zhí mín dì (殖民地 colony)

dāng (当 at; then) + dì (地 land) = dāng dì (当地 local)

gēng (耕 plough) + dì (地 land) = gēng dì (耕地 plough; plantation)

jī (基 base; basic) + dì (地 site) = jī dì (基地 base;)

dì (地 situation) + bù (步 step) = dì bù (地步 situation)

发 fā

1. deliver; send out; disperse

2. issue; launch

3. become; turn

4. grow; flourish

考试热词 HOT WORDS FOR TESTS

fā (发 issue) + biǎo (表 express) = fā biǎo (发表 publish; announce)

fā (发 issue) + bù (布 notify) = fā bù (发布 issue; release)

fā (发 issue) + chóu (愁 worry; anxious) = fā chóu (发愁 worry; be anxious)

fā (发 issue) + dāi (呆 dull; stagnate) = fā dāi (发呆 be in a daze; absence of mind)

fā (发 issue) + shēng (生 born; generate) = fā shēng (发生 happen)

fā (发 deliver) + huī (挥 disperse; wield) = fā huī (发挥 give play to; play a role)

fā (发 issue) + dǒu (抖 shake) = fā dǒu (发抖 shiver; tremble)

fā (发 issue) + míng (明 light; clear-sighted) = fā míng (发明 invent)

fā (发 issue) + piào (票 ticket) = fā piào (发票 invoice)

fā (发 become) + jué (觉 feel; sense) = fā jué (发觉 realize; find)

fā (发 become; turn) + shāo (烧 burn) = fā shāo (发烧 have a fever)

fā (发 launch) + shè (射 shoot) = fā shè (发射 launch)

fā (发 launch) + shì (誓 swear) = fā shì (发誓 swear; vow)

fā (发 launch) + dòng (动 move) = fā dòng (发动 launch; issue)

fā (发 launch) + xíng (行 go) = fā xíng (发行 issue; distribute)

qǐ (启 start; open) + fā (发 launch) = qǐ fā (启发 enlighten; inspire)

zì (自 self) + fā (发 launch) = zì fā (自发 spontaneous)
bào (爆 explode) + fā (发 launch) = bào fā (爆发 break out; outburst)
bèng (迸 burst out; burst forth) + fā (发 launch) = bèng fā (迸发 burst out)
kāi (开 open) + fā (发 launch) = kāi fā (开发 develop)
pī (批 batch) + fā (发 launch) = pī fā (批发 wholesale; sale by bulk)
jī (激 stimulate) + fā (发 launch) = jī fā (激发 motivate; stimulate)
fā (发 issue) + yán (言 word; say) = fā yán (发言 speak; make a statement)
bān (颁 confer; promulgate) + fā (发 issue) = bān fā (颁发 issue; promulgate)
fā (发 become; turn) + yán (炎 inflame; infected) = fā yán (炎 inflame; irritated)
fā (发 become; turn) + xiàn (现 appear) = fā xiàn (发现 discover; find)
fā (发 disperse) + yáng (扬 raise; spread) = fā yáng (发扬 carry forward)
fā (发 grow) + yù (育 raise; bring up) = fā yù (发育 growth; up growth)
fā (发 grow) + zhǎn (展 extend) = fā zhǎn (发展 develop)
sàn (散 spread) + fā (发 disperse) = sàn fā (散发 disperse; spread)
zhēng (蒸 steam) + fā (发 disperse) = zhēng fā (蒸发 evaporate; evaporation)
fā (发 flourish) + dá (达 distinguish) = fā dá (发达 prosperous; developed)
fā (发 flourish) + cái (财 fortune) = fā cái (发财 become rich)
shā (沙) + fā (发) = shā fā (沙发 sofa, a onomatopoetic word for "sofa")

发 fà

hair

考试热词 HOT WORDS FOR TESTS

tóu (头 head) + fà (发 hair) = tóu fa (头发 hair)
lǐ (理 manage) + fà (发 hair) = lǐ fà (理发 haircut; hair dress)

爱 ài

love; like; be in fond of

考试热词 HOT WORDS FOR TESTS

ài (爱 love) + dài (戴 put on; honor) = ài dài (爱戴 love and esteem; respect and support)

ài (爱 love) + hào (好 like) = ài hào (爱好 hobby; appetite)

ài (爱 love) + hù (护 protect) = ài hù (爱护 care; cherish)

ài (爱 love) + qíng (情 feeling; emotion) = ài qíng (爱情 love)

ài (爱 love) + xī (惜 cherish) = ài xī (爱惜 cherish; value; treasure)

ài (爱 love) + xīn (心 heart) = ài xīn (爱心 love; compassion)

kě (可 dependable; acceptable) + ài (爱 love) = kě ài (可爱 cute; lovely; adorable)

rè (热 hot) + ài (爱 love) = rè ài (热爱 ardently love)

téng (疼 be very fond of) + ài (爱 love) = téng ài (疼爱 love dearly; set one's affection on sb)

liàn (恋 love) + ài (爱 love) = liàn ài (恋爱 be in love)

安 ān

1. quiet; calm

2. safe; security

3. to secure; to calm

4. install; arrange

考试热词 HOT WORDS FOR TESTS

ān (安 quiet) + jìng (静 quiet) = ān jìng (安静 quiet)

ān (安 quiet) + níng (宁 peaceful) = ān níng (安宁 quiet; peaceful)

ān (安 arrange) + pái (排 arrange) = ān pái (安排 arrange; schedule)

ān (安 safe) + quán (全 entire; complete) = ān quán (安全 safe; security)

ān (安 to calm) + wèi (慰 condole) = ān wèi (安慰 comfort)

ān (安 quiet) + xiáng (详 serene) = ān xiáng (安详 serene; unruffled)

ān (安 install) + zhì (置 put; place) = ān zhì (安置 install, arrange for)

ān (安 install) + zhuāng (装 install) = ān zhuāng (安装 install)

zhì (治 govern, manage) + ān (安 security) = zhì ān (治安 public security)

bú (不 no; not) + ān (安 calm; quiet) = bù ān (不安 uneasy)

gōng (公 public) + ān (安 safe; security) = gōng ān (公安 public security)

gōng ān (公安 public security) + jú (局 bureau) = gōng ān jú (公安局 public security bureau)

出 chū

1. go (come) out; leave
2. exceed; go beyond
3. issue; publish
4. appear; put forth
5. payout; expend

考试热词 HOT WORDS FOR TESTS

chū (出 issue) + bǎn (版 edition; version) = chū bǎn (出版 publish)

chū (出 go; leave) + chāi (差 business) = chū chāi (出差 be on a business trip)

chū (出 go; leave) + fā (发 dispatch; send) = chū fā (出发 go; leave)

chū (出 go; leave) + lù (路 road) = chū lù (出路 outlet; way-out)

chū (出 leave) + mài (卖 sell) = chū mài (出卖 sell; betray)

chū (出 exceed) + sè (色 color) = chū sè (出色 excellent; distinguish)

chū (出 come out) + shēn (身 body) = chū shēn (出身 family background)

chū (出 go out) + shén (神 spirit; soul) = chū shén (出神 trance; abstraction)

chū (出 go out) + shēng (生 born; live) = chū shēng (出生 born; birth)

chū (出 come out) + shì (示 show) = chū shì (出示 show; present)

chū (出 go out) + xī (息 rest; interest) = chū xī (出息 prospects; future)

chū (出 come out) + xí (席 position; chair) = chū xí (出席 attend)

chū (出 come out) + xiàn (现 appear) = chū xiàn (出现 appear)

chū (出 go out) + zū (租 rent) = chū zū (出租 rent out)

chū zū (出租 rent out) + chē (车 vehicle; car) = chū zū chē (出租车 cab; taxi)

jié (杰 marvelous) + chū (出 exceed) = jié chū (杰出 outstanding; marvelous)

yǎn (演 show; performance) + chū (出 go out) = yǎn chū (演出 show; performance)

tū (突 bulge; abruptly) + chū (出 exceed) = tū chū (突出 extrude; stand out)

zhī (支 spend) + chū (出 pay out) = zhī chū (支出 pay; spend)

céng (层 layer) + chū (出 come out) + bú (不 no) + qióng (穷 end; finish) = céng chū bù qióng (层出不穷 emerge in endlessly)

005

Behind the Curtain

Mechanism of Generating Vocabulary

Though each of the languages has its unique method to build up its vocabulary system, that method is always based on the common sense and knowledge of the people who are using that language. A language is a tool for all people and for everyday use, and this fact actually decides that the grammar of a language can never be based on some obscure theories created by some theorists. Believe me, if you are frustrated by something from a grammar book, you need not to feel guilty because it is not your fault.

The method for words-creation in the Chinese language is easy to understand. Think about what you would do when you are trying to find something on an on-line shopping website: You will input several keywords and then will find a list suggested. In case you find nothing after browsing several pages, you would try other more accurate keywords, or try to add more keywords to those ones you previously used. The most likely result would be that you would get a more accurate list, and if you are lucky, your favorite thing would be on the top.

In fact, the reason beneath the above example is totally same

On-line shopping really brings great convenience to people's everyday life.

to that in the words-creation process in the Chinese language. To put it simply, people select two (or more) element words, which function the same as the "keywords", thus to form a combination to be a "new" word for an object. In appearance, it looks like people add one character with the other to build a "new" word.

With a deeper view, this way of creating words is based on a procedure of "Analyzing, Selecting, and Optimizing". When people need to create a word for an object, they would first analyze the typical features of it. Of course, some features are common ones while some are specific ones, and all these features are like labels stick on that object. What people need to do is to select minimum features as long as they can differentiate the object from others. That's is why most of the words listed in the dictionary are formed by two or three characters. One important thing during that creative process is that: Everything is based on common sense and knowledge, and only in this way, the words can be accepted by all speakers.

For convenience of our upcoming discussion, we define this

method based on that mechanism as the "Combining Method". The following example can help to explain this method well. When a new machine, train, appeared in the eyes of the Chinese people, the first thing they did was to create a name for that. There were many possibilities, and undoubtedly, this machine was a type of vehicle, and it has many other typical features like "fast", "huge", "coal burning", "steel", "steam", "smoke", "fire" , etc. Finally people used a features combination by "fire (火 , huǒ)" and "vehicle (车 chē)" thus creating a new word, 火车 (huǒ chē) for this machine.

Here are some other examples:

shōu (收 collect; receive) + yīn (音 sound; tone) + jī (机 machine) = shōu yīn jī (收音机 radio)

zhào (照 lighten; photograph) + xiàng (相 image; picture) + jī (机 machine) = zhào xiàng jī (照相机 camera)

xǐ (洗 wash) + yī (衣 clothes) + jī (机 machine) = xǐyī jī (洗衣机 washing machine; washer)

It is quite interesting that the procedure of creating a word is performed by group decision, and it frequent happens that people would create various words for the same object. For example, in Chinese, there two popular words for computers:

jìsuàn (计算 calculate; count) + jī (机 machine) = jì suàn jī (计算机 computer)

diàn (电 electricity) + nǎo (脑 brain) =diàn nǎo (电脑 computer)

There is one more thing to note: In many cases, the words created by the combining method have more than one meaning. Anyway, compared with those elements words, these words are much more simplified in both meaning and function. Here are some examples:

bào (报 report; reward) + xiāo (销 eliminate; erase) = bào xiāo (报销 reimburse; destroy; finish)

shén (神 soul; god) + jīng (经 channel; longitude) = shén jīng (神经 nerve; lunatic; psychotic)

WORDS BANK

In many cases, learners get their understanding of the meanings and functions of the element words (characters) by way of learning words that are created by the combining method.

心 xīn

1. heart
2. mind; soul
3. center; core

考试热词 HOT WORDS FOR TESTS

xīn (心 heart) + dé (得 get; gain) = xīn dé (心得 experience; understanding)
xīn (心 heart) + lǐ (理 reason; sense) = xīn lǐ (心理 mentality; psychology)
xīn (心 heart) + líng (灵 soul) = xīn líng (心灵 soul; spirit)
xīn (心 heart) + qíng (情 emotion) = xīn qíng (心情 emotion)
xīn (心 heart) + tài (态 status) = xīn tài (心态 mentality; attitude)
xīn (心 heart) + téng (疼 ache) = xīn téng (心疼 distressed; love dearly)
xīn (心 heart) + xuè (血 blood) = xuè (心血 painstaking effort)
xīn (心 heart) + yǎn (眼 eye; hole) + ér (儿 suffix) = xīn yǎnr (心眼儿 smart; tactful)
xīn (心 heart) + zàng (脏 organ) = xīn zàng (心脏 heart)
yě (野 wild) + xīn (心 heart) = yě xīn (野心 wild ambition)
zhōng (中 center) + xīn (心 center) = zhōng xīn (中心 center; core)
zhōng (衷 sincere) + xīn (心 heart) = zhōng xīn (衷心 sincere; sincerely)
zhuān (专 special; specific) + xīn (心 mind) = zhuān xīn (专心 concentrate; attend to)
cāo (操 do; handle) + xīn (心 mind) = cāo xīn (操心 worry about)
chéng (成 deliberate) + xīn (心 mind) = chéng xīn (成心 intentionally; on purpose)
cū (粗 thick; coarse) + xīn (心 mind) = cū xīn (粗心 careless; thoughtless)
dān (担 carry) + xīn (心 mind) = dān xīn (担心 worry about)
dāng (当 at; on) + xīn (心 mind) = dāng xīn (当心 be careful; look out)
diǎn (点 spot; dot) + xīn (心 heart) = diǎn xin (点心 dessert; dim sum)

ě (恶 sick; lousy) + xīn (心 heart) = ě xīn (恶心 sick; lousy)

fàng (放 lay; put) + xīn (心 heart) = fàng xīn (放心 be at ease; feel relieved)

guān (关 about; related) + xīn (心 mind) = guān xīn (关心 care for; concern)

hé (核 core) + xīn (心 heart) = hé xīn (核心 core)

huī (灰 gray) + xīn (心 mind) = huī xīn (灰心 discouraged)

jīng (精 refined; extractive) + xīn (心 mind) = jīng xīn (精心 elaborately; meticulously)

jué (决 decide) + xīn (心 mind) = jué xīn (决心 determination; decision)

kāi (开 open) + xīn (心 mind) = kāi xīn (开心 happy)

liáng (良 good) + xīn (心 mind) = liáng xīn (良心 conscientiousness)

nài (耐 durance; durable) + xīn (心 mind) = nài xīn (耐心 patience)

rè (热 warm) + xīn (心 heart) = rè xīn (热心 earnest; ardent)

shāng (伤 injure; injured) + xīn (心 heart) = shāng xīn (伤心 sad; heart-broken)

xiǎo (小 small; little) + xīn (心 mind) = xiǎo xīn (小心 be careful; be cautious)

xū (虚 empty; humble) + xīn (心 mind) = xū xīn (虚心 modest; open-minded)

xīn (心 heart) + gān (甘 willingness) + qíng (情 emotion) + yuàn (愿 wish; adore) = xīn gān qíng yuàn (心甘情愿 be most willing to; with full willingness)

xiǎo (小 small) + xīn (心 mind) + yì (翼 wing) + yì (翼 wing) = xiǎo xīn yì yì (小心翼翼 gingerliness; scrupulousness)

qí (齐 together) + xīn (心 mind) + xié (协 joint; assist) + lì (力 power; strength) = qí xīn xié lì (齐 心 协 力 make concerted effort; pull together)

chèn (称 fit) + xīn (心 mind) + rú (如 like; as) + yì (意 will; willingness) = chèn xīn rú yì (称心如意 well-content; after one's own heart)

名 míng

1. name; title

2. fame; reputation

3. describe; express

3. famous; well-known

考试热词 HOT WORDS FOR TESTS

míng (名 title) + cì (次 order) = míng cì (名次 ranking)

míng (名 name) + é (额 quantity) = míng é (名额 the number of candidate allowed) míng (名 famous) + pái (牌 plate; brand) = míng pái (名牌 famous brand)

míng (名 name) + piàn (片 piece) = míng piàn (名片 name card)

míng (名 fame) + yù (誉 reputation) = míng yù (名誉 reputation)

míng (名 name) + zì (字 title) = míng zi (名字 name)

bào (报 report, inform) + míng (名 name) = bào míng (报名 register; enroll)

mìng (命 order; command) + míng (名 name) = mìng míng (命名 to name; denominate)

yǒu (有 have) + míng (名 fame) = yǒu míng (有名 famous)

zhù (著 famous) + míng (名 fame) = zhù míng (著名 famous)

mò (莫 no; not) + míng (名 express) + qí (其 it; that) + miào (妙 reason; subtle) = mò míng qí miào (莫名其妙 without rhyme or reason; odd)

míng (名 famous) + shèng (胜 outstanding) + gǔ (古 ancient; old) + jì (迹 relics) = míng shèng gǔ jì (名胜古迹 scenic spots and historical sites)

míng (名 fame; tile) + fù (副 match; fit) + qí (其 it; that) + shí (实 reality; truth) = míng fù qí shí (名副其实 be worthy of the name)

面 miàn

1. face; surface; cover

2. side; top; aspect

3. scope; area; range

4. (wheat) powder; noodle

5. soft; tender

6. to face; be in front of

考试热词 HOT WORDS FOR TESTS

miàn (面 wheat powder) + bāo (包 package; bun) = miàn bāo (面包 bread)

miàn (面 to face) + duì (对 towards; to) = miàn duì (面对 to face)

miàn (面 area) + jī (积 sum; total) = miàn jī (面积 area)

miàn (面 to face) + lín (临 near; nearby) = miàn lín (面临 face to)

miàn (面 face) + mào (貌 appearance) = miàn mào (面貌 out looking; appearance)

miàn (面 wheat powder) + tiáo (条 stripe) = miàn tiáo (面条 noodle)

miàn (面 face) + zǐ (子 suffix) = miàn zi (面子 face; dignity)

biǎo (表 outside; surface) + miàn (面 surface) = biǎo miàn (表面 surface)

cè (侧 side) + miàn (面 face; surface) = cè miàn (侧面 flank; side face)

chǎng (场 field) + miàn (面 surface) = chǎng miàn (场面 scene; occasion)

dāng (当 at; on) + miàn (面 face) = dāng miàn (当面 face to face)

duì (对 opposite) + miàn (面 face; side) = duì miàn (对面 opposite; right in front)

fǎn (反 reverse) + miàn (面 face; side) = fǎn miàn (反面 reverse side; wrong side)

fāng (方 direction) + miàn (面 scope) = fāng miàn (方面 aspect; field)

hòu (后 rear; back) + miàn (面 side) = hòu mian (后面 rear; back)

jiàn (见 see; meet) + miàn (面 face) = jiàn miàn (见面 meet; face)

jú (局 situation) + miàn (面 surface) = jú miàn (局面 situation; scene)

piàn (片 piece) + miàn (面 scope) = piàn miàn (片面 one-sided; unilateral)

qián (前 front) + miàn (面 side) = qián mian (前面 front)

quán (全 all; entire) + miàn (面 scope) = quán miàn (全面 comprehensive; overall)

shū (书 book; literal) + miàn (面 surface) = shū miàn (书面 in written form)

yíng (迎 meet; receive) + miàn (面 face) = yíng miàn (迎面 head-on; bow-on)

机 jī

1. chance; opportunity

2. machine; vehicle; engine

3. organic

4. adroit; ingenious

5. key issues; secrets

6. reason; mechanism

考试热词 HOT WORDS FOR TESTS

jī (机 machine) + dòng (动 move; act) = jī (机动 maneuvering; engine driven)

jī (机 machine) + qì (器 vehicle) = jī qì (机器 machine)

jī (机 machine) + xiè (械 tool) = jī xiè (机械 machine)

fēi (飞 fly) + jī (机 machine) = fēi jī (飞机 airplane)

jī (机 machine) + chǎng (场 field) = jī chǎng (机场 airport)

dēng (登 climb; get on board) + jī (机 machine) = dēng jī (登机 boarding; go a board)

dēng jī (登机 boarding) + pái (牌 plate) = dēng jī pái (登机牌 boarding pass; boarding card)

sī (司 manage; control) + jī (机 machine) = sī jī (司机 driver)

jī (机 chance) + huì (会 meet) = jī huì (机会 opportunity; chance)

jī (机 chance) + yù (遇 meet) = jī yù (机遇 opportunity)

shí (时 time) + jī (机 chance) = shí jī (时机 opportunity; occasion)

tóu (投 cast; send) + jī (机 chance) = tóu jī (投机 speculate; be opportunistic)

wēi (危 danger) + jī (机 chance) = wēi jī (危机 crisis; conjuncture)

jī (机 ingenious) + líng (灵 smart) = jī ling (机灵 clever; ingenious)

jī (机 adroit) + zhì (智 wisdom) = jī zhì (机智 smart; tact)

dòng (动 move; act) + jī (机 reason; cause) = dòng jī (动机 motivation; intention)

jī (机 organic) + gòu (构 structure) = jī gòu (机构 organization)

jī (机 mechanism) + mì (密 secret) = jī mì (机密 confidential)

时 shí

1. time; day; period
2. hour
3. opportunity; chance

考试热词 HOT WORDS FOR TESTS

shí (时 time) + chā (差 difference) = shí chā (时差 time lag)

shí (时 time) + cháng (常 usual) = shí cháng (时常 usually)

shí (时 time) + dài (代 generation) = shí dài (时代 times; generation)

shí (时 time) + ér (而 and; but) = shí ér (时而 sometimes; now and then)

shí (时 time) + guāng (光 light) = shí guāng (时光 time)

shí (时 time) + hòu (候 season) = shí hou (时候 (the duration of) time; occasion)

shí (时 time) + jiān (间 space; separation) = shí jiān (时间 time)

shí (时 time) + kè (刻 moment) = shí kè (时刻 time; moment)

shí (时 time) + máo (髦 fine long hair) = shí máo (时髦 vogue; fashion; fashionable)

shí (时 time) + qī (期 period) = shí qī (时期 period)

shí (时 time) + shàng (尚 adore; fond) = shí shàng (时尚 fashion; fashionable)
shí (时 time) + shì (事 matter; affair) = shí shì (时事 current affair)
zàn (暂 temporary) + shí (时 time) = zàn shí (暂时 temporarily; for the moment)
zhǔn (准 accurate; exact) + shí (时 time) = zhǔn shí (准时 on time; punctuality)
àn (按 according; follow) + shí (时 time) = àn shí (按时 on schedule; on time)
bú (不 no; not) + shí (时 time) = bù shí (不时 from time to time; often)
dāng (当 at on) + shí (时 time) = dāng shí (当时 at that time; then)
dùn (顿 suddenly; pause) + shí (时 time) = dùn shí (顿时 at once; immediately)
jí (及 reach) + shí (时 time) = jí shí (及时 timely; in time)
lín (临 arrive; just before) + shí (时 time) = lín shí (临时 temporary)

器 qì

1. implement; ware; utensil
2. capacity
3. organ

考试热词 HOT WORDS FOR TESTS

wǔ (武 military) + qì (器 implement) = wǔ qì (武器 weapon)
yí (仪 instrument) + qì (器 utensil) = yí qì (仪器 apparatus; instrument)
lè (乐 music) + qì (器 utensil) = yuè qì (乐器 musical instrument)
chōng (充 fill) + diàn (电 electricity) + qì (器 utensil) = chōng diàn qì (充电器 charger)
qì (器 organ) + guān (官 organ) = qì guān (器官 organ)
róng (容 contain) + qì (器 utensil) = róng qì (容器 vessel; container)

006

Ways of Nature

Three Basic Meaning-Generating Types

Until now, you probably realized that the essence in the combining method is to generate another meaning by the interaction of two (or more) origin ones. So it would be very important to understand the rules in this course. For it would help you to easily catch the results from the magical method, or to understand numerous words without any painful rote memorization.

Don't think that we are going into some profound theories, on the contrary, everything that happens in the meaning-generating course is in accordance to common sense in our everyday life. The following examples will help you to understand the three basic types of how a "new" meaning is created from the combining process.

Think about the couples around you. If we put them into categories according to the similarity between the husband and wife, we will probably put them into three major types:

The first type is like this: They have almost everything in common: the fondness of food, sports, the style of clothes, etc... In one word, they are the shadow of each other.

The same situation also happens in the combining process: Two origin words with the same (or almost same) meanings are combined to make a word, which have the same meaning to the original ones. For example:

péng (朋 friend) + yǒu (友 friend) = péng you (朋友 friend)

Here we denominate this meaning-generating type as the "Coincidental Type", and the following chart shows the interaction of the meanings. For the convenience for discussion in coming contents, we give a code as "T-1" for it.

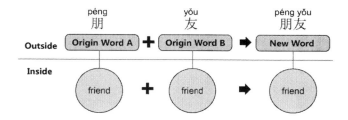

The second type of couples are like this: They have totally different personalities and habits. One likes to stay calm and be alone while the other like to stay in a noisy crowd. One like to go shopping while the other thinks it is torture. It seems that they always stay in opposite poles of the world. In the Chinese language, there is an interesting word for couples like that: yuān jiā (冤家 foe). But it is amazing that many marriages like this are sustained for a life-long time. The same situation also happens in the combining process: Two origin words with the opposite (or almost opposite) meanings are combined to make a word. However, in many cases, the final meaning usually refers to a general concept related to the original meanings. For example:

shēn (深 deep; profound) + qiǎn (浅 shallow; simple) = shēn qiǎn (深浅 depth; complexity)

sǐ (死 dead) + huó (活 alive) = sǐ huó (死活 fate; plight)

Here we denominate this meaning-generating type as the "Opposite Type", and the following chart shows the interaction of the meanings. For the convenience for discussion in coming contents, we give a code as "T-2" for it.

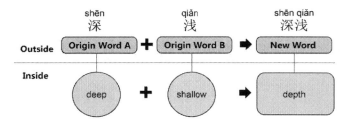

The third type seems much more popular among couples: They are not same nor opposite to each other, but just different. One likes go shopping, and the other likes reading but never hates to go shopping together with the other. With mutual compromising and integrating, the differences bring fun and newness to each of the couples. The same situation also happens in the combining process: Two origin words with different meanings are combined to make a word with an integrated meaning. For example:

chī (吃 eat; have) + jīng (惊 shock) = chī jīng (吃惊 shocked; be surprised)

chī (吃 eat; have) + lì (力 power; strength) = chī lì (吃力 strenuous; laborious)

Here we denominate this meaning-generating type as the "Integrated Type", and the following chart shows the interaction of the meanings. For the convenience for discussion in coming contents, we give a code as "T-3" for it.

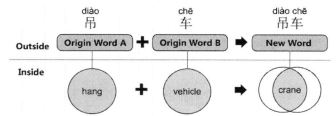

One thing to note is that, the above three types show the most fundamental cases in the meaning-generating process. Meanwhile, in many cases, an origin word might have several different meanings and functions. When it is combined with other ones, the meaning-generating process could be based on any one of these three basic types.

WORDS BANK

For beginners, it might be a little bit difficult to figure out that which meaning of an origin word is used during a combining process, and in which type the final meaning comes out. A simpler way is to use a method of exclusion, and it is something like playing a puzzle: You need to find the right way to integrate the two pieces.

报 bào

1. newspaper
2. report; declare
3. reward; recompense
4. revenge

HOT WORDS FOR TESTS

bào (报 newspaper) + shè (社 press) = bào shè (报社 newspaper office)

bào (报 report) + dào (到 arrive) = bào dào (报到 check in; register)

bào (报 report) + dào (道 say; express) = bào dào (报道 report (by news media))

yù (预 in advance) + bào (报 report) = yù bào (预报 forecast)

bào (报 declare) + jǐng (警 warn; warning) = bào jǐng (报警 alarm; call the police)

bào (报 report) + zhǐ (纸 paper) = bào zhǐ (报纸 newspaper)

bào (报 revenge) + chóu (仇 spouse) = bào chóu (报仇 revenge)

bào (报 report) + gào (告 tell) = bào gào (报告 report; inform)

huì (汇 gather) + bào (报 report) = huì bào (汇报 report; inform)

shēn (申 apply) + bào (报 report) = shēn bào (申报 declare; declaration)

qíng (情 situation) + bào (报 report) = qíng bào (情报 information)

bào (报 reward) + chóu (酬 reward) = bào chóu (报酬 reward; payment)

huí (回 return) + bào (报 reward) = huí bào (回报 Payback)

bào (报 recompense) + dá (答 reply) = bào dá (报答 pay back)

bào (报 recompense) + xiāo (销 cancel) = bào xiāo (报销 reimburse; reimbursement)

bào (报 revenge) + fù (复 reply; backward) = bào fù (报复 retaliate)

周 zhōu

1. week
2. circumference; around
3. complete; thorough

考试热词 HOT WORDS FOR TESTS

zhōu (周 week) + mò (末 end) = zhōu mò (周末 weekend)

zhōu (周 around) + biān (边 side) = zhōu biān (周边 rim; circum)

zhōu (周 around) + wéi (围 surround) = zhōu wéi (周围 around; periphery)

zhōu (周 around) + zhé (折 fold) = zhōu zhé (周折 twists and turns; setbacks)

zhōu (周 around) + zhuǎn (转 roll) = zhōu zhuǎn (周转 turnover; revolve)

zhōu (周 thorough) + dào (到 reach) = zhōu dào (周到 considerate; thorough)

zhōu (周 thorough) + mì (密 intensive) = zhōu mì (周密 careful; thorough)

zhōu (周 complete) + nián (年 year) = zhōu nián (周年 anniversary)

zhōu (周 complete) + qī (期 period) = zhōu qī (周期 cycle; cyclicality)

zhòng (众 crowd) + suǒ (所 that) + zhōu (周 thorough) + zhī (知 know) = zhòng suǒ zhōu zhī (众所周知 as everyone knows)

照 zhào

1. photograph
2. according to
3. illuminate; shine; enlighten
4. license
5. take care; concern

考试热词 HOT WORDS FOR TESTS

zhào (照 photograph) + piàn (片 piece) = zhào piàn (照片 photo)

zhào (照 according to) + cháng (常 routine; usual) = zhào cháng (照常 as usual)

zhào (照 according to) + yàng (样 sample) = zhào yàng (照样 all the same)

àn (按 according to) + zhào (照 according to) = àn zhào (按照 according to)

cān (参 reference) + zhào (照 according to) = cān zhào (参照 refer to)
duì (对 compare) + zhào (照 according to) = duì zhào (对照 compare; comparison)
zhào (照 enlighten) + yào (耀 shine) = zhào yào (照耀 enlighten)
zhào (照 take care) + gù (顾 care) = zhào gù (照顾 take care)
guān (关 care) + zhào (照 concern) = guān zhào (关照 take care of)
zhí (执 execute) + zhào (照 license) = zhí zhào (执照 license; certification)
hù (护 protect) + zhào (照 license) = hù zhào (护照 passport)

规 guī

1. rule; regulation
2. plan; procedure
3. advise
4. gauge

考试热词 HOT WORDS FOR TESTS

guī (规 rule) + dìng (定 rule) = guī dìng (规定 rule)
guī (规 rule) + fàn (范 model) = guī fàn (规范 standard; specification)
guī (规 rule) + jǔ (矩 rule) = guī ju (规矩 rule; discipline)
guī (规 rule) + lǜ (律 rule) = guī lǜ (规律 regular pattern)
guī (规 rule) + zé (则 rule) = guī zé (规则 rule; regulation)
guī (规 rule) + zhāng (章 chapter) = guī zhāng (规章 regulations)
zhèng (正 right; upright) + guī (规 rule) = zhèng guī (正规 regular; standard)
guī (规 gauge) + gé (格 grade) = guī gé (规格 specification; norms)
guī (规 gauge) + mó (模 scale) = guī mó (规模 scale)
guī (规 plan) + huà (划 deploy) = guī huà (规划 plan; programming)

意 yì

1. mean; meaning
2. wish; desire; expect; expectation
3. opinion; view; idea

4. be aware of; thinking; care

考试热词 HOT WORDS FOR TESTS

yì (意 opinion) + jiàn (见 view) = yì jiàn (意见 opinion; idea)

yì (意 be aware of) + shí (识 recognize) = yì shí (意识 consciousness; mentality)

zhù (注 input; note) + yì (意 be aware of) = zhù yì (注意 notice; pay attention to)

yì (意 meaning) + sī (思 thinking) = yì si (意思 meaning; intention)

yì (意 meaning) + wèi (味 flavor) = yì wèi (意味 mean; signify)

yì (意 meaning) + yì (义 meaning) = yì yì (意义 meaning)

yì (意 expect) + tú (图 desire) = yì tú (意图 intention; purpose)

yì (意 thinking) + wài (外 exceed; outside) = yì wài (意外 by accident)

zài (在 at; on) + yì (意 thinking) = zài yì (在意 care; take notice of)

yì (意 think) + liào (料 speculate) = yì liào (意料 speculate; think)

yì (意 desire) + xiàng (向 direction) = yì xiàng (意向 intention)

dé (得 get; gain) + yì (意 desire) = dé yì (得意 proud; complacent)

yì (意 wish) + zhì (志 wish) = yì zhì (意志 will, willingness)

yuàn (愿 wish) + yì (意 wish) = yuàn yì (愿意 wish to; agree to)

tè (特 specific) + yì (意 wish) = tè yì (特意 particular; particularly)

gù (故 cause; reason) + yì (意 wish) = gù yì (故意 on purpose; deliberately)

zhǔ (主 host) + yì (意 idea) = zhú yi (主意 idea)

dà (大 big) + yì (意 care) = dà yì (大意 main points; careless)

tóng (同 same; with) + yì (意 opinion) = tóng yì (同意 agree)

wán (玩 play) + yì (意 care) + ér (儿 a suffix) = wán yìr (玩意儿 gadget)

事 shì

1. matter; case; affair

2. job; business

3. work on

考试热词 HOT WORDS FOR TESTS

shì (事 matter) + gù (故 disappear; vanish) = shì gù (事故 accident)
gù (故 past) + shì (事 matter) = gù shi (故事 story)
shì (事 matter) + jì (迹 trace) = shì jì (事迹 deed; story)
shì (事 matter) + jiàn (件 piece) = shì jiàn (事件 case; affaire)
shì (事 matter) + qíng (情 situation) = shì qíng (事情 matter)
shì (事 matter) + shí (实 truth) = shì shí (事实 truth)
shì (事 matter) + tài (态 status) = shì tài (事态 situation)
shì (事 business) + wù (务 business) = shì wù (事务 business)
shì (事 matter) + wù (物 object) = shì wù (事物 objects)
shì (事 matter) + xiān (先 advance) = shì xiān (事先 in advance)
shì (事 business) + xiàng (项 item) = shì xiàng (事项 matter; items)
shì (事 business) + yè (业 business) = shì yè (事业 business; undertaking)
tóng (同 same) + shì (事 job) = tóng shì (同事 colleague)
wǎng (往 past) + shì (事 matter) = wǎng shì (往事 the past; history)
xíng (刑 punishment) + shì (事 mater) = xíng shì (刑事 criminal)
běn (本 root) + shì (事 job) = běn shi (本事 skill; ability)
shī (失 lost) + shì (事 matter) = shī shì (失事 wreck; wreckage)
cóng (从 follow) + shì (事 work on) = cóng shì (从事 work on; engage)
jūn (军 army) + shì (事 matter) = jūn shì (军事 military)
lǐng (领 adopt; lead) + shì (事 matter) = lǐng shì (领事 consul)
lǐng shì (领事 consul) + guǎn (馆 hall) = lǐng shì guǎn (领事馆 consulate)
qǐ (启 start) + shì (事 matter) = qǐ shì (启事 notice; announcement)

007

It Makes Sense

The Principle of "Rationality"

Undoubtedly, the combining method brings unlimited possibilities in creating "new" words for this language. However, a coin always has two sides. A potential problem with this method is that it might generate excessive words if used without control, and what is more, it might produce some "private" words created in strong personal preferences. All these would destroy the efficiency of the language. So people should find some way to control the "side effects" of this powerful tool, to prevent the creation of a personal private language within the language.

During the long period of evolution of the Chinese language, people established some effective principles and rules in applying that powerful tool. The most basic one is the Principle of Rationality, which means that the creation process should be based on the rational logics and common knowledge of most users. This principle actually guarantees that a "new" word can be easily understood and applied by most of the native speakers.

Here is an example. The element word, 流 (liú, stream; flow), refers to a typical action of "flowing". With the combining method, people can use it to create words for many objects that have the essential feature of "flowing".

> shuǐ (水 , water) + liú(流 , current; flow) = shuǐliú (水流 water flow)
>
> ní (泥 mud) + shí (石 stone) + 流 (liú, current flow) = ní shí liú (泥石流 debris flow)

Another example is another 铁流 (tiě liú, iron flow). It means "the armored troops moving". Regardless, you will rarely encounter the words like 果流 (guǒ liú) or 书流 (shū liú) just because there is no such like objects commonly used in

people's everyday life.

For many Mandarin Chinese learners, there might be some problems. Sometimes, they have enough reason to be sure that they are using some "good" words while those words actually are not acceptable in everyday language. For example:

> diàn (电 electricity) + dào (道 way; road) = diàn dào (电道 ~~Unacceptable!)
>
> diàn (电 electricity) + lù (路 route; way) = diàn lù (电路 circuit)
>
> sī (思 think; thoughts) + dào (道 way; road) = sī dào

51

(思道 ~~Unacceptable!)

sī (思 think; thoughts) + lù (路 route; way) = sī lù (思路 way of thinking)

dì (地 land; earth) + dào (道 way; road) = dì dào (地道 tunnel)

dì (地 land; earth) + lù (路 route; way) = dì lù (地路 ~~Unacceptable!)

The fact is that people would really only use 电路, 思路 and 地道 in their everyday language, and the words like 电道, 思道 and 地路 are totally unacceptable. The preferences in selecting words is largely decided by the subtle differences in the meanings of element words. Anyway, it is really a shame that, even a native speaker cannot always explain well when facing a questions like "Why it should be this, not that?"

词汇仓库
WORDS BANK

Thanks to the Principle of Rationality, in most cases, learners can successfully "guess" the finial meanings of the words created by the combining method. But sometimes, the "meaning addition" game does not work well, and one reason is that some words have drifted from their original meanings over the years. So in this case, the only way is to memorize them.

气 qì

1. gas; air

2. breath; spirit; morale

3. weather

4. manner; style

5. insult; bully

6. get angry; enrage

考试热词 HOT WORDS FOR TESTS

qì (气 air) + fēn (氛 atmosphere) = qì fēn (气氛 atmosphere; aura)

qì (气 air) + wèi (味 smell; flavor) = qì wèi (气味 smell; odor)

qì (气 air) + yā (压 press; pressure) = qì yā (气压 air pressure)

yǎng (氧 oxygen) + qì (气 air) = yǎng qì (氧气 oxygen)

yùn (运 fortune;) + qì (气 air) = yùn qi (运气 luck; fortune)

fú (福 happiness) + qì (气 air) = fú qi (福气 good fortune)

yǔ (语 language; word) + qì (气 air) = yǔ qì (语气 tone; mood) xiè (泄 discharge; release) + qì (气 air) = xiè qì (泄气 staleness; lose heart)

qì (气 breath) + gōng (功 function) = qì gōng (气功 qigong; controlled breathing exercise)

chuǎn (喘 puff; pant) + qì (气 breath) = chuǎn qì (喘气 pant; gasp)

fú (服 be convinced) + qì (气 breath) = fú qi (服气 be convinced)

tàn (叹 sigh; acclaim) + qì (气 breath) = tàn qì (叹气 sigh)

qì (气 weather) + hòu (候 season) = qì hòu (气候 climate)

qì (气 weather) + xiàng (象 appearance; feature) = qì xiàng (气象 weather; atmosphere)

qì (气 spirit) + gài (概 deportment) = qì gài (气概 spirit; mettle)

qì (气 spirit) + pò (魄 soul) = qì pò (气魄 courage; boldness of vision)

qì (气 sprite) + sè (色 color) = qì sè (气色 complexion)

jiāo (娇 charming; frail) + qì (气 spirit) = jiāo qì (娇气 delicacy; effeminacy)

qì (气 spirit) + shì (势 situation; trend) = qì shì (气势 vigor; momentum)

qì (气 spirit) + zhì (质 quality) = qì zhì (气质 temperament)

lì (力 strength) + qì (气 spirit) = lì qi (力气 strength; effort)

yǒng (勇 brave) + qì (气 spirit) = yǒng qì (勇气 courage)

táo (淘 naughty) + qì (气 spirit) = táo qì (淘气 naughty)

zhāo (朝 morning) + qì (气 spirit) + péng (蓬 fluffy) + bó (勃 erect) = zhāo qì péng bó (朝气蓬勃 full of youthful spirit)

zhēng (争 fight; strive) + qì (气 spirit) = zhēng qì (争气 try to win credit for)

zhèng (正 right; positive) + qì (气 spirit) = zhèng qì (正气 uprightness; rectitude)

zhì (志 willingness) + qì (气 spirit) = zhì qì (志气 ambition; aspiration)

xiǎo (小 small) + qì (气 spirit) = xiǎo qi (小气 stingy; penny-pinching)

lǐ (理 reason) + zhí (直 straight) + qì (气 breath) + zhuàng (壮 strong) = lǐ zhí qì zhuàng (理直气壮 walk tall; righteous)

pí (脾 spleen) + qì (气 breath) = pí qi (脾气 temper; temperament)

kè (客 guest) + qì (气 manner) = kè qi (客气 polite; stand on scruples)

bú (不 no; not) + kè qì (客气 polite) = bú kè qi (不客气 blunt; You're welcome)

体 tǐ

1. body; object; substance

2. style; form

3. experience (sth)

考试热词 HOT WORDS FOR TESTS

shēn (身 body) + tǐ (体 body) = shēn tǐ (身体 body)

tǐ (体 body) + yù (育 cultivate; education) = tǐ yù (体育 sports; physical education)

shī (尸 corpse) + tǐ (体 body) = shī tǐ (尸体 corpse; dead body)

dà (大 big) + tǐ (体 substance) = dà tǐ (大体 in general; on the whole)

tǐ (体 body) + miàn (面 face) = tǐ miàn (体面 dignity; grace)

tǐ (体 body) + tiē (贴 paste) = tǐ tiē (体贴 considerate; care about)

tǐ (体 body) + jī (积 sum; volume) = tǐ jī (体积 volume; dimension)

tǐ (体 body) + xì (系 system) = tǐ xì (体系 system)

yè (液 liquid) + tǐ (体 body) = yè tǐ (液体 liquid)

zhěng (整 entire) + tǐ (体 body) = zhěng tǐ (整体 overall; entirety)

gè (个 individual) + tǐ (体 body) = gè tǐ (个体 individual)

jí (集 gather) + tǐ (体 body) = jí tǐ (集体 collective; collectivity)

tuán (团 group) + tǐ (体 body) = tuán tǐ (团体 organization; group)

jiě (解 unbind; separate) + tǐ (体 body) = jiě tǐ (解体 break up; disassembly)

jù (具 specific) + tǐ (体 body) = jù tǐ (具体 specific; definite)

lì (立 erect) + tǐ (体 body) = lì tǐ (立体 three-dimensional)

méi (媒 media) + tǐ (体 body) = méi tǐ (媒体 media; medium)

tǐ (体 style; form) + cái (裁 style; form) = tǐ cái (体裁 literature form)

fán (繁 complicated) + tǐ (体 style) + zì (字 letter) = fán tǐ zì (繁体字 traditional Chinese character)

jiǎn (简 simple) + tǐ (体 style) + zì (字 letter) = jiǎn tǐ zì (简体字 simplified Chinese character)

tǐ (体 experience) + huì (会 understand) = tǐ huì (体会 experience; realize)

tǐ (体 experience) + yàn (验 investigate) = tǐ yàn (体验 experience)

tǐ (体 experience) + xiàn (现 appear) = tǐ xiàn (体现 embody; reflect)

tǐ (体 experience) + liàng (谅 forgive) = tǐ liàng (体谅 allow for; understand)

书 shū

1. book

2. write; record

考试热词 HOT WORDS FOR TESTS

shū (书 book) + jí (籍 book; records) = shū jí (书籍 book)
shū (书 book) + jià (架 shelf) = shū jià (书架 bookshelf)
tú (图 picture) + shū (书 book) = tú shū (图书 books)
tú shū (图书 books) + guǎn (馆 hall) = tú shū guǎn (图书馆 library)
zhèng (证 prove) + shū (书 book) = zhèng shū (证书 certificate)
shū (书 write) + fǎ (法 method; way) = shū fǎ (书法 calligraphy)
mì (秘 secret) + shū (书 write) = mì shū (秘书 secretary)
shū (书 write) + jì (记 record) = shū jì (书记 secretary)

天 tiān

1. sky; universe
2. day; date
3. natural; inherent

考试热词 HOT WORDS FOR TESTS

tiān (天 sky) + kōng (空 space) = tiān kōng (天空 sky; space)
tiān (天 sky) + qì (气 air) = tiān qì (天气 weather)
tiān (天 sky) + wén (文 rule) = tiān wén (天文 astronomy)
zuó (昨 past) + tiān (天 day) = zuó tiān (昨天 yesterday)
jīn (今 now; present) + tiān (天 day) = jīn tiān (今天 today; nowadays)
míng (明 tomorrow) + tiān (天 day) = míng tiān (明天 tomorrow)
lǐ bài (礼拜 worship; pray) + tiān (天 day) = lǐ bài tiān (礼拜天 Sunday)
tiān (天 sky) + táng (堂 hall) = tiān táng (天堂 heaven)
háng (航 sail; voyage) + tiān (天 sky) = háng tiān (航天 spaceflight)
liáo (聊 talk) + tiān (天 sky) = liáo tiān (聊天 chat; chitchat)
tiān rán (天然) + qì (气 air) = tiān rán qì (天然气 natural gas)
tiān (天 natural) + cái (才 gift; talent) = tiān cái (天才 genius)
tiān (天 natural) + fù (赋 endow) = tiān fù (天赋 talent; innate skill)
tiān (天 natural) + shēng (生 born) = tiān shēng (天生 born; innate)

tiān (天 natural) + zhēn (真 real) = tiān zhēn (天真 innocent; naive)

dé (得 get; have) + tiān (天 natural) + dú (独 only) + hòu (厚 thick; rich) = dé tiān dú hòu (得天独厚 be richly endowed by nature)

tiān (天 natural) + lún (伦 order; relation) + zhī (之 of) + lè (乐 happy) = tiān lún zhī lè (天伦之乐 family happiness)

风 fēng

1. wind
2. style; manner

考试热词 HOT WORDS FOR TESTS

bào (暴 violent) + fēng (风 wind) = bào fēng (暴风 storm)

guā (刮 blow) + fēng (风 wind) = guā fēng (刮风 wind blowing)

tái fēng (台风 an onomatopoetic word for typhoon)

fēng (风 wind) + guāng (光 light; bright) = fēng guāng (风光 scenery; glorious)

fēng (风 wind) + jǐng (景 scene) = fēng jǐng (风景 landscape; scenery)

fēng (风 wind) + xiǎn (险 danger) = fēng xiǎn (风险 risk)

fēng (风 style) + dù (度 degree; extent) = fēng dù (风度 demeanor; presence)

fēng (风 style) + gé (格 style) = fēng gé (风格 character; style)

fēng (风 style) + qì (气 atmosphere) = fēng qì (风气 custom; ethos)

fēng (风 style) + qù (趣 fun; funny) = fēng qù (风趣 wit; humor)

fēng (风 style) + sú (俗 tradition) = fēng sú (风俗 custom; convention)

fēng (风 style) + wèi (味 flavor) = fēng wèi (风味 relish; special flavor)

zuò (作 do; behave) + fēng (风 style) = zuò fēng (作风 style; way)

wēi (威 might; strength) + fēng (风 style) = wēi fēng (威风 power and prestige)

008

The Hidden Center

The Principle of "Core-in-End"

In Section 006, we discussed the three basic meaning-generation types: Coincidental Type (T-1, Example Word: 朋友), Opposite Type (T-2, Example word: 深浅) and Integrated Type (T-2, Example word: 吃惊). In T-3, a popular way to create a "new" word is to combine one origin word referring to an essential feature with the other referring to a specific feature. For example:

fēi (飞 fly) + jī (机 machine; vehicle) = fēi jī (飞机 airplane)

In a specific combining course, the origin word referring to the essential features is called the "Core Word". In the above example, jī(机 machine; vehicle) is the core word because it describes the essential feature of the complicated machinery. In the combining courses based on T-3, in case there is an obvious core word, the core word should always be put at the end of the combination. That's the Principle of Core-in-End. If you insist on raising a question as to "Why the core word should be put at the end?" I can only say that it might be something related to the popular habits of Chinese people. They like saving money, and they want to leave the best part at the end.

The reason for introducing this principle is that, in most cases, the reverse combining sequence will result in an incorrect word. For example:

cān (餐 food; meal) + tīng (厅 hall; lobby) = cān tīng (餐厅 restaurant)

tīng (厅 hall; lobby) + cān (餐 food; meal) = tīng cān (厅餐 ~~Unacceptable!)

bìng (病 sick; ill) + dú (毒 poison) = bìng dú (病毒 virus)

dú (毒 poison) + bìng (病 sick; ill) = dú bìng (病毒 ~~Unacceptable!)

In some cases, a reverse combining sequence can also result in a "good" word, but mostly with a completely different meaning. For example:

带 (dài, lead; tie) + 领 (lǐng, lead; collar) = 带领 (lead)

领 (lǐng, lead; collar) + 带 (dài, lead; tie)= 领带 (a tie)

Even though a reverse combining sequent might result in a "good" word, it is till based on the principle of "Rationality Coherence". For the combining course based on T-3, it should follow the principle of the "Core-in-End". The following are some typical examples:

fēng (蜂 , bee) + mì (蜜 honey) = fēng mì (蜂蜜 honey)
mì (蜜 honey) + fēng (蜂 , bee) = mì fēng (蜜蜂 honeybee)
běn (本 root; original) + rén (人 people; human) = běn rén (本人 oneself)
rén (人 people; human) + běn (本 root; original) = rén běn (人本 human-oriented; humanism)
biàn (变 change; transfer) + zhì (质 quality) = biàn zhì (变质 go bad; deteriorate)
zhì (质 quality) + biàn (变 change; transfer) = zhì biàn (质变 metamorphosis; transmutation)
chǎn (产 produce) + liàng (量 quantity) = chǎn liàng (产量 yield; output)
liàng (量 quantity) + chǎn (产 produce) = liàng chǎn (量产 mass production)
chéng (成 become; portion) + fèn (分 element) = chéng fèn (成分 element; ingredient)
fēn (分 divide; separate) + chéng (成 become; portion) = fēn chéng (分成 divide into; dividend)
chéng (成 complete; all) + tiān (天 sky; day) = chéng tiān (成天 all day long)
tiān (天 sky; day) + chéng (成 complete; all) = tiān chéng (天成 natural)
chéng (成 grow; complete) + zhǎng (长 grow) = chéng zhǎng (成长 grow)
长 (zhǎng, grow) + chéng (成 grow; complete) = chéng zhǎng (长成 grow into; mature)
chū (出 out) + mài (卖 sell) = chū mài (出卖 betray)
mài (卖 sell) + chū (出 out) = mài chū (卖出 sell; selling)
chuán (传 pass; inherit) + zhēn (真 real; reality) = chuán zhēn (传真 fax)
zhēn (真 real; reality) + chuán (传 pass; inherit) = zhēn chuán (真传 authentic)
chuǎn (喘 pant; asthma) + qì (气 gas; air) = chuǎn qì (喘气 pant)
qì (气 gas; air) + chuǎn (喘 pant; asthma) = qì chuǎn (气喘 asthma; short of breath)
dā (答 answer; reply) + yìng (应 reply; agree) = dā yìng (答应 agree; promise)

yìng (应 reply; agree) + dá (答 answer; reply) = yìng dá (应答 response; reply)

dǎ (打 hit) + jī (击 attack; hit) = dǎ jī (打击 attack; strike)

jī (击 attack; hit) + dǎ (打 hit) = jī dǎ (击打 hit; beat)

dǎo (导 guide) + xiàng (向 direction) = dǎo xiàng (导向 lead to; oriented)

xiàng (向 direction) + dǎo (导 guide) = xiàng dǎo (向导 guide (person))

dào (到 arrive; go to) + dá (达 reach) = dào dá (到达 arrive)

dá (达 reach) + dào (到 arrive; go to) = dá dào (达到 reach; reach to)

dòng (动 move) + jī (机 machine; occasion) = dòng jī (动机 intention; motivation)

jī (机 machine; occasion) + dòng (动 move) = jī dòng (机动 maneuver; maneuvering)

dòng (动 move) + mài (脉, pulse) = dòng mài (动脉 artery)

mài (脉, pulse) + dòng (动 move) = mài dòng (脉动 pulsation; impulse)

dù (度 spend; degree) + guò (过 pass; over) = dù guò (度过 spend (time))

guò (过 pass; over) + dù (度 spend; degree) = guò dù (过度 excessive; excessively)

duì (对 face; counter) + miàn (面 face; face to) = duì miàn (对面 opposite)

miàn (面 face; face to) + duì (对 face; counter) = miàn duì (面对 face to; confront)

duì (对 face; counter) + yīng (应 response; correspond) = duì yīng (对应 correspond; corresponding)

yìng (应 correspond; corresponding) + duì (对 face; counter) = yìng duì (应对 answer; deal with)

fā (发 issue; send out) + huī (挥 wave; disperse) = fā huī (发挥 give play to)

huī (挥 wave; disperse) + fā (发 issue; send out) = huī fā (挥发 disperse; volatilize)

nián (年 year) + jì (纪 age) = nián jì (年纪 age)

jì (纪 record) + nián (年 year) = jì nián (纪年 calendar era)

nǚ (女 female) + ér (儿 kid) = nǚ ér (女儿 daughter)

ér (儿 son) + nǚ (女 daughter) = ér nǚ (儿女 kids; children)

qī (期 period) + xiàn (限 limitation) = qī xiàn (期限 time limitation)

xiàn (限 limit) + qī (期 period) = xiàn qī (限期 within a definite time)

ài (爱 love) + qíng (情 emotion) = ài qíng (爱情 love)
qíng (情 emotion) + ài (爱 love) = qíng ài (情爱 affection)

chū (出 go out) + fā (发 launch) = chū fā (出发 leave)
fā (发 launch) + chū (出 out) = fā chū (发出 issue; give out)

gǎn (感 feel) + dòng (动 move) = gǎn dòng (感动 affect; touch)
dòng (动 move) + gǎn (感 feeling) = dòng gǎn (动感 sporty; dynamic)

gē (歌 sing) + sòng (颂 praise) = gē sòng (歌颂 eulogize)
sòng (颂 praise) + gē (歌 song) = sòng gē (颂歌 ode)

gǔ (骨 bone) + tóu (头 a suffix) = gǔ tou (骨头 bone)
tóu (头 head) + gǔ (骨 bone) = tóu gǔ (头骨 skull)

guó (国 nation) + wáng (王 king) = guó wáng (国王 king)
wáng (王 king) + guó (国 nation) = wáng guó (王国 kingdom)

hé (和 peace) + píng (平 calm) = hé píng (和平 peace)
píng (平 peaceful) + hé (和 amicable) = píng hé (平和 gentle; mild)

hòu (后 back) + bèi (背 back of body) = hòu bèi (后背 back of body)
bèi (背 back) + hòu (后 back) = bèi hòu (背后 behind; at the back)

huà (化 become) + shí (石 stone) = huà shí (化石 fossil)
shí (石 stone) + huà (化 convert; -ize) = shí huà (石化 petrifaction)

huáng (黄 yellow) + hūn (昏 dusk) = huáng hūn (黄昏 nightfall)
hūn (昏 dim) + huáng (黄 yellow) = hūn huáng (昏黄 pale yellow)

huáng (黄 yellow) + jīn (金 gold) = huáng jīn (黄金 gold)
jīn (金 gold) + huáng (黄 yellow) = jīn huáng (金黄 golden)

huì (会 meeting) + yì (议 discussion) = huì yì (会议 meeting)
yì (议 discussion) + huì (会 meeting) = yì huì (议会 congress; parliament)

jī (基 basic) + dì (地 land) = jī dì (基地 base)
dì (地 land) + jī (基 base) = dì jī (地基 foundation; base)

009

Stages of Growth

The Principle of "One-off Functioning"

Using the combining method, Chinese people can create unlimited basic words with limited characters (origin words). Meanwhile, people should still control the side-effect of the method; creating too many words. Too many words will also harm the efficiency of communication. That's why the quantity of the words listed in dictionaries remain relatively stable, and it happens in almost every language.

The fact is that, there are too many things and concepts in the world, which definitely go far beyond the range of words in any dictionary. People need to build words for each of them, and a popular way, almost in every language in the world, is to make combinations based on the limited quantities of basic words. Here is an example:

dǎ yìn (打印 print) + jī (机 machine) = dǎ yìn jī (打印机 a printer)

cǎi sè (彩色 color) + dǎ yìn jī (打印机 printer) = cǎi sè dǎ yìn jī (彩色打印机 a color printer)

jīguāng (激光 laser) + cǎi sè dǎ yìn jī (彩色打印机 color printer) = jīguāng cǎi sè dǎ yìn jī (激光彩色机 a laser color printer)

There is no surprise that the Chinese language also use the combining method to meet the demands for words. But one unique thing is that, all the principles and rules for creating basic words are also applicable for creating complicated words. Here is a more complicated example:

The Chinese word for this snack is:

lǎo běi jīng fēng wèi shāo bǐng (老北京风味烧饼)

This long word is generated by several combining course, and here are the combining courses involved:

Step 1:

lǎo (老 , old) + Běijīng (北京 Beijing) = lǎo běi jīng (老北京 old Beijing) (T-3)

Step 2:

fēng (风 wind; style) + wèi (味 flavor) = fēng wèi

(风味 local flavor) (T-3)

Step 3:

shāo (烧 burn) + bǐng (饼 cookie; pastry) = shāo bǐng (烧饼 baked pastry) (T-3)

Step 4:

lǎo běi jīng (老北京 old Beijing) + fēng wèi (风味 local flavor) = lǎo běi jīng fēng wèi (老北京风味 flavor of Old Beijing) (T-3)

Step 5:

lǎo běi jīng fēng wèi (老北京风味 flavor of Old Beijing) + shāo bǐng (烧饼 baked pastry) = lǎo běi jīng fēng wèi shāo bǐng (老北京风味烧饼 A baked pastry with traditional flavor of Beijing) (T-3)

The following chart might help you understand the process.

In each of the Steps 1, 2 and 3, we get a basic word by combining two origin words, while in Step 4 and Step 5, we get two complex words with the same combining method.

One thing to be noted is that, another principle plays an important role in creating such complex words, which is called the principle of "One-off Functioning". It means that each of the words as materials will lose its original meaning and function, and the combination should be regarded as an independent word with its own meaning and function. In other words, after "participating" in a combing course to create a "new word", an origin word will have no influence to the further combining course between the "new word" and the others.

Maybe a famous chemical experiment can help you to understand this process better. Oxygen burns with hydrogen, and then the reaction results in a new element; water, which has its own features and usages. After burning the materials, oxygen and hydrogen lose their original appearances and functions. When we use the water to make a cup of coffee or tea, we do not consider any connection to those gases.

The most important advantage brought by the "One-off Functioning" principle is that it makes the meaning-generating course go in a distinct and highly structured way, especially in the case of creating complicated words. To put it more simply, this principle makes everything go in a simplistic way like "1+1=2".

Generally speaking, most everyday words, including basic words and complex words, are constructed by two or three characters.

考试热词 HOT WORDS FOR TESTS

bǐ (笔 pen) + jì (记 record) = bǐ jì (笔记 note)

bǐ jì (笔记 note) + běn (本 book) = bǐ jì běn (笔记本 notebook)

bàn (办 do) + gōng (公 public) = bàn gōng (办公 do business)

bàn gōng (办公 do business) + shì (室 room) = bàn gōng shì (办公室 office)

nǎo (脑 brain) + jīn (筋 tendon) = nǎo jīn (脑筋 brain; head)

shāng(伤) + nǎo jīn (脑筋 brain; head) = shāng nǎo jīn (伤脑筋 headache; bother)

tài (太 extreme) + jí (极 end; pole) = tài jí (太极 Taiji; Tai Chi)

tài jí (太极 Taiji; Tai Chi) + quán (拳 fist) = tài jí quán (太极拳 Taiji martial)

gāng (钢 steel) + qín (琴 musical instrument) = gāng qín (钢琴 piano)

tán (弹 flip) +gāng qín (钢琴 piano) = tán gāng qín (弹钢琴 play piano)

zú (足 foot) + qiú (球 ball) = zú qiú (足球 football; soccer)

tī (踢 kick) + zú qiú (足球 football; soccer) = tī zú qiú (踢足球 play soccer)

xià (夏 summer) + lìng (令 season) = xià lìng (夏令 summer)

xià lìng (夏令 summer) + yíng (营 camp) = xià lìng yíng (夏令营 summer camp)

yuán (元 first; beginning) + xiāo (宵 night) = yuán xiāo (元宵 the night of the 15th of the first lunar month; Lanterns)

yuán xiāo (元宵 Lanterns) + jié (节 festival) = yuán xiāo jié (元宵节 festival of Lanterns)

zì (自 self; by oneself) + xíng (行 go; move) = zì xíng (自行 by oneself)

zì xíng (自行 by oneself) + chē (车 vehicle) = zì xíng chē (自行车 bicycle)

bó (博 broad) + lǎn (览 view) = bó lǎn (博览 broad view; read extensively)

bó lǎn (博览 broad view; read extensively) + huì (会 meeting) = bó lǎn huì (博览会 expo; fair) bó (博 broad) + wù (物 object) = bó wù (博物 mass objects)

bó wù (博物 mass objects) + guǎn (馆 hall) = bó wù guǎn (博物馆 museum)

bèi (备 prepare; prevent) + wàng (忘 forget) = bèi wàng (备忘 remind)

bèi wàng (备忘 remind) + lù (录 record) = bèi wàng lù (备忘录 memo)

dà (大 big; giant) + shǐ (使 envoy) = dà shǐ (大使 ambassador)

dà shǐ (大使 ambassador) + guǎn (馆 hall) = dà shí guǎn (大使馆 embassy)

dǎn (胆 courage) + xiǎo (小 small; little) = dǎn xiǎo (胆小 timid; cowardice)

dǎn xiǎo (胆小 timid; cowardice) + guǐ (鬼 ghost) = dǎn xiáo guǐ (胆小鬼 coward)

jiāo (交 interact) + dào (道 way; path) = jiāo dào (交道 contact)

dǎ (打 do; make; play) + jiāo dào (交道 contact) = dǎ jiāo dào (打交道 deal with)

diàn (电 electricity) + huà (话 words; dialogue) = diàn huà (电话 telephone)

dǎ (打 do; make; play) + diàn huà (电话 telephone) = dǎ diàn huà (打电话 make a phone call)

dàn (蛋 egg) + bái (白 white) = dàn bái (蛋白 egg white)

dàn bái (蛋白 egg white) + zhì (质 material; quality) = dàn bái zhì (蛋白质 protein)

guān (官 official; administration) + sī (司 command; judge) = guān si (官司 lawsuit)

dǎ (打 do; make; play) + guān si (官司 lawsuit) = dǎ guān si (打官司 litigate; engage in a lawsuit)

lán (篮 basket) + qiú (球 ball) = lán qiú (篮球 basketball)

dǎ (打 do; make; play) + lán qiú (蓝球 basketball) = dǎ lán qiú (打篮球 play basketball)

zhāo (招 attract) + hū (呼 call) = zhāo hu (招呼 call; greeting)

dǎ (打 do; make; play) + zhāo hu (招呼 call; greeting) = dǎ zhāo hu (打招呼 greet sb.)

duō (多 many; much) + yuán (元 dimension) = duō yuán (多元 multivariate)

duō yuán (多元 multivariate) + huà (化 become; -ize) = duō yuán huà (多元化 diversification)

shǔ (暑 summer) + jià (假 vacation) = shǔ jià (暑假 summer vacation)

fàng (放 issue; launch) + shǔ jià (暑假 summer vacation) = fàng shǔ jià (放暑假 have a summer vacation)

huǒ (火 fire) + chē (车 vehicle) = huǒ chē (火车 train)

huǒ chē (火车 train) + zhàn (站 station) = huǒ chē zhàn (火车站 railway station) hù (互 mutual) + lián (联 connect) = hù lián (互联 mutual connecting)

hù lián (互联 mutual connecting) + wǎng (网 net) = hù lián wǎng (互联网 Internet)

lì (立 stand) + jiāo (交 cross) = lì jiāo (立交 interchange)

lì jiāo (立交 interchange) + qiáo (桥 bridge) = lì jiāo qiáo (立交桥 overpass; interchange)

lǐ (里 mile) + chéng (程 distance) = lǐ chéng (里程 mileage)

lǐ chéng (里程 mileage) + bēi (碑 stone tablet) = lǐ chéng bēi (里程碑 milestone)

shòu (售 sell) + huò (货 commodity; goods) = shòu huò (售货 sell goods)

shòu huò (售货 sell goods) + yuán (员 person) = shòu huò yuán (售货员 salesclerk; salesman)

sù (塑 mould) + liào (料 material) = sù liào (塑料 plastic)

sù liào (塑料 plastic) + dài (袋 bag) = sù liào dài (塑料袋 plastic bag)

wèi (卫 keep; protect) + shēng (生 life) = wèi shēng (卫生 sanitation)

wèi shēng (卫生 sanitation) + jiān (间 room) = wèi shēng jiān (卫生间 bathroom)

yǔ (羽 feather) + máo (毛 fur) = yǔ máo (羽毛 feather)

yǔ máo (羽毛 feather) + qiú (球 ball) = yǔ máo qiú (羽毛球 badminton)

yǔ (羽 feather) + róng (绒 fine hair) = yǔ róng (羽绒 down feather)

yǔ róng (羽绒 down feather) + fú (服 clothing; suit) = yǔ róng (羽绒服 down jacket; down wear)

zhǐ (指 point) + nán (南 south) = zhǐ nán (指南 guide; south indicating)

zhǐ nán (指南 guide; south indicating) + zhēn (针 needle) = zhǐ nán zhēn (指南针 compass)

zhì (志 will; wish) + yuàn (愿 will; willingness) = zhì yuàn (志愿 wish; volunteering)

zhì yuàn (志愿 wish; volunteering) + zhě (者 people; individual) = zhì yuàn zhě (志愿者 volunteer)

gāo (高 high) + sù (速 speed) = gāo sù (高速 high speed)

gōng (公 public) + lù (路 road) = gōng lù (公路 road; highway)

gāo sù (高速 high speed) + gōng lù (公路 road) = gāo sù gōng lù (高速公路 express way)

gōng (公 public) + gòng (共 public) = gōng gòng (公共 public)

qì (汽 gas) + chē (车 vehicle) = qì chē (汽车 vehicle; car)

gōng gòng (公共 public) + qì chē (汽车 vehicle; car) = gōng gòng qì chē (公共汽车 bus)

010

Blurry Borderlines

Basic Words, Complex Words, and Phrases

As we discussed before, words are the most fundamental units in a language, and as a whole, they mirror the numerous objects and concepts in our lives.

These words that refer to the elementary objects and concepts are called "Basic Words". In English, you can easily figure them out because they are listed as independent terms in a dictionary, with specific and unique appearances, definitions, and pronunciations. But in the Chinese language, things are little bit confusing. On one hand, almost all the characters (origin words) are basic words, and on the other hand, by the combining method, a huge amount of basic words are created. For example, the following words are all basic words:

    hǎi (海 sea; ocean) + bá (拔 raise) = hǎi bá (海拔 elevation)

    hǎi (海 sea; ocean) + yáng (洋 ocean) = hǎi yáng (海洋 ocean)

To create words for objects or concepts with more specific, or unique features, a popular way is to make combinations by using the basic words, and it happens in almost all the languages. The words created in this way are "Complex Words", which usually would not be enrolled in a dictionary, and people would build them as need. Here are some examples for complex words:

    dà (大 big) + yǔ (雨 rain) = dà yǔ (大雨 heavy rain)

    xiǎo (小 small) + yǔ (雨 rain) = xiáo yǔ (小雨 light rain)

    hǎo (好 good) + rén (人 people; human) = hǎo rén (好人 good person; good guy)

    huài (坏 bad) + rén (人 people; human) = huài rén (坏人 bad person; bad guy)

In English, it quite easy to differentiate the basic words and complex words, while in Chinese, it is a little bit difficult because you can never tell the difference between a basic word and a complex word. In both cases, they are built up by two origin words.

You might see a concept such as "Phrases" in some grammar books. Generally speaking, phrases could be regarded as a specific type of complex words which have more complicated meanings and appearances as well. Anyhow, in Chinese language, the essence of building a complicated phrase is repetitive applications of the combining method.

An interesting fact is that there is not a distinct borderline between the families of basic words and complex words, and the same situation happens to the complex words and phrases. Here is an example:

    1. gē (歌 sing; song)

    2. chàng (唱 sing)

3. gē chàng (歌唱 to sing)

4. gē chàng jiā (歌唱家 singer)

5. nǚ gē chàng jiā (女歌唱家 female singer)

6. zhù míng nǚ gē chàng jiā (著名女歌唱家 a famous female singer)

7. zhōngguó zhù míng nǚ gē chàng jiā (中国著名女歌唱家 a famous Chinese female singer)

In the above words, the words from the first to fourth are usually classified as basic words. But with the fifth, there would be a debate in whether it is a basic word or not. For the last two ones, there also would be some arguments as to whether they are complex words or phrases. A fact is that few Chinese native speakers care about the differences between them. My personal suggestion is that you don't worry about such disturbances. The most important thing for you is to grasp the skills to understand all the results and what's more important, learn how to create the things you want.

WORDS BANK

Theoretically speaking, the meaning of a word that is generated by the combining method usually has logical connections with the meanings of the origin words. But, sometimes, there are no obvious connections between them. One of the reasons for this is that the meanings change largely during the long-term evolution of the language.

保 bǎo
1. protect; defend
2. keep; maintain
3. guarantee; assure

HOT WORDS FOR TESTS

bǎo (保 protect) + hù (护 protect) = bǎo hù (保护 protect)
bǎo (保 protect) + mǔ (姆 wet nurse) = bǎo mǔ (保姆 baby-sitter; servant)
bǎo (保 protect) + wèi (卫 protect) = bǎo wèi (保卫 protect; defend)
bǎo (保 protect) + yǎng (养 maintain) = báo yǎng (保养 maintain; maintenance)
bǎo (保 protect) + zhàng (障 barrier) = bǎo zhàng (保障 guarantee; protection)
bǎo (保 defend) + xiǎn (险 risk) = báo xiǎn (保险 insurance)
bǎo (保 keep) + chí (持 maintain) = bǎo chí (保持 keep; maintain)
bǎo (保 keep) + cún (存 save; keep) = bǎo cún (保存 keep; store)
bǎo (保 keep) + guǎn (管 manage) = báo guǎn (保管 keep; custody)
bǎo (保 keep) + liú (留 stay; remain) = bǎo liú (保留 retain; reserve)
bǎo (保 keep) + mì (密 secret) = bǎo mì (保密 keep secret)
bǎo (保 keep) + shǒu (守 guard) = báo shǒu (保守 guard; conservative)
bǎo (保 keep) + zhèng (证 prove) = bǎo zhèng (保证 ensure; warranty)
dān (担 carry) + bǎo (保 guarantee) = dān bǎo (担保 guarantee; assurance)
què (确 assure) + bǎo (保 assure) = què bǎo (确保 ensure; make sure)

表 biǎo

1. watch; meter
2. surface; outside
3. example; model
4. form; chart
5. show; express

HOT WORDS FOR TESTS

biǎo (表 outside) + qíng (情 emotion) = biǎo qíng (表情 expression; face)

wài (外 outside) + biǎo (表 surface) = wài biǎo (外表 surface; appearance)

biǎo (表 express) + dá (达 reach) = biǎo dá (表达 express; convey)

biǎo (表 express) + jué (决 decide) = biǎo jué (表决 vote; take a vote)

biǎo (表 express) + míng (明 clear; distinct) = biǎo míng (表明 indicate; declare)

biǎo (表 express) + shì (示 show) = biǎo shì (表示 express; signify)

biǎo (表 express) + tài (态 attitude) = biǎo tài (表态 declare; take a stand)

biǎo (表 express) + xiàn (现 appear) = biǎo xiàn (表现 performance; presentation)

biǎo (表 express) + yǎn (演 show; perform) = biáo yǎn (表演 perform; performance)

biǎo (表 express) + yáng (扬 raise; spread) = biǎo yáng (表扬 praise; commend)

biǎo (表 express) + zhāng (彰 clear; show) = biǎo zhāng (表彰 commend; honor)

dài (代 represent) + biǎo (表 express) = dài biǎo (代表 on behalf of; representative)

biǎo (表 form; chart) + gé (格 grid) = biǎo gé (表格 form; sheet)

包 bāo

1. wrap; include; contain; surround
2. undertake; take full charge of
3. assure; guarantee
4. bag; package

HOT WORDS FOR TESTS

bāo (包 wrap) + zhuāng (装 hold; install) = bāo zhuāng (包装 pack; package)

bāo (包 wrap) + zǐ (子 a suffix) = bāo zi (包子 steamed stuffed bun; Bao zi)
bāo (包 include) + hán (含 include) = bāo hán (包含 include; contain)
bāo (包 include) + kuò (括 include) = bāo kuò (包括 include; cover)
bāo (包 surround) + wéi (围 surround) = bāo wéi (包围 surround; encircle)
bāo (包 undertake) + bì (庇 asylum; shield) = bāo bì (包庇 shield; cover up)
chéng (承 carry) + bāo (包 undertake) = chéng bāo (承包 contract with; undertake)
bāo (包 package) + fú (袱 package) = bāo fu (包袱 bundle; burden)
bāo (包 package) + guǒ (裹 wrap) = bāo guǒ (包裹 parcel; package)
dǎ (打 make; do) + bāo (包 package) = dǎ bāo (打包 bale; pack)

成 chéng

1. established; ready-made; fully grown

2. accomplish; accomplishment

3. succeed; success

3. become, turn into

考试热词 HOT WORDS FOR TESTS

chéng (成 established) + yǔ (语 language; words) = chéng yǔ (成语 idiom)
chéng (成 established) + yuán (员 body; member) = chéng yuán (成员 member)
xiàn (现 now) + chéng (成 established) = xiàn chéng (现成 ready-made; available)
chéng (成 accomplishment) + běn (本 cost) = chéng běn (成本 cost)
chéng (成 accomplishment) + fèn (分 element) = chéng fèn (成分 ingredient; composition)
chéng (成 accomplish) + shú (熟 mature) = chéng shu (成熟 ripen; mature)
wán (完 finish) + chéng (成 accomplish) = wán chéng (完成 finish; complete)
zàn (赞 praise) + chéng (成 accomplish) = zàn chéng (赞成 approve of; endorse)
chéng (成 accomplish) + lì (立 stand; erect) = chéng lì (成立 establish; found)
chéng (成 succeed) + gōng (功 achievement) = chéng gōng (成功 success; succeed)
chéng (成 succeed) + guǒ (果 fruit) = chéng guǒ (成果 achievement; outcome)
chéng (成 succeed) + jī (绩 merit; achievement) = chéng jī (成绩 result; score; achievement)
chéng (成 succeed) + jiù (就 accomplishment) = chéng jiù (成就 achievement; attainment)

chéng (成 succeed) + xiào (效 effect) = chéng xiào (成效 effect; efficiency)

chéng (成 succeed) + jiāo (交 interact) = chéng jiāo (成交 closing the deal)

dá (达 reach) + chéng (成 succeed) = dá chéng (达成 reach; conclude)

chéng (成 become) + wéi (为 be) = chéng wéi (成为 become; get)

gòu (构 construct) + chéng (成 become) = gòu chéng (构成 form; constitute)

hé (合 integrate) + chéng (成 become) = hé chéng (合成 compound; composite)

luò (落 fall) + chéng (成 become) = luò chéng (落成 completed; completion)

xíng (形 form) + chéng (成 become) = xíng chéng (形成 form; come into being)

zǔ (组 organize) + chéng (成 become) = zǔ chéng (组成 constitute; make up; compose)

yǎng (养 cultivate; nourish) + chéng (成 become) = yǎng chéng (养成 cultivate; develop)

zào (造 make) + chéng (成 become) = zào chéng (造成 give rise to; cause)

光 guāng

1. light; ray; brightness

2. bright; honor; glory

3. favor; grace

4. smooth

考试热词 HOT WORDS FOR TESTS

yáng (阳 sun) + guāng (光 light) = yáng guāng (阳光 sunlight)

bào (曝 expose) + guāng (光 light) = bào guāng (曝光 expose; make public)

guāng (光 light) + máng (芒 awn) = guāng máng (光芒 ray of light)

yǎn (眼 eye) + guāng (光 light) = yǎn guāng (眼光 vision; foresight; taste)

guān (观 see; watch) + guāng (光 light) = guān guāng (观光 sightseeing)

guāng (光 light) + pán (盘 disk) = guāng pán (光盘 compact disc; CD)

guāng (光 bright) + míng (明 bright) = guāng míng (光明 bright; brightness)

guāng (光 bright) + cǎi (彩 color; colorful) = guāng cǎi (光彩 shine; glory)

guāng (光 glory) + huī (辉 brilliance) = guāng huī (光辉 brilliance; brilliant)

guāng (光 honor) + róng (荣 honor) = guāng róng (光荣 glory; honor)

zhān (沾 touch; soak) + guāng (光 favor) = zhān guāng (沾光 benefit from association with sb. or sth)

guāng (光 favor) + lín (临 arrive) = guāng lín (光临 presence (of a guest, customer, etc))
guāng (光 smooth) + huá (滑 slip; slippery) = guāng huá (滑 smooth; glazing)

解 jiě

1. untie; dismiss;

2. relieve; settle; solve

3. divide; separate; melt

4. explain; interpret

5. understand; perceive

考试热词 HOT WORDS FOR TESTS

jiě (解 untie) + gù (雇 hire) = jiě gù (解雇 lay off; fire)
jiě (解 dismiss) + sàn (散 spread) = jiě sàn (解散 dismiss)
wǎ (瓦 tile) + jiě (解 separate) = wǎ jiě (瓦解 collapse; disintegrate)
jiě (解 relieve) + fàng (放 release) = jiě fàng (解放 liberate)
jiě (解 solve) + chú (除 eliminate) = jiě chú (解除 dismiss; relieve)
huǎn (缓 relax; mitigate) + jiě (解 relieve) = huǎn jiě (缓解 ease; remit)
fēn (分 separate) + jiě (解 divide) = fēn jiě (分解 resolve; decompose)
róng (溶 dissolve) + jiě (解 melt) = róng jiě (溶解 dissolve; dissolution)
jiě (解 divide) + pōu (剖 dissect) = jiě pōu (解剖 dissect; dissection)
jiě (解 explain) + shì (释 explain) = jiě shì (解释 explain)
biàn (辩 debate; argue) + jiě (解 explain) = biàn jiě (辩解 argue; excuse)
lǐ (理 understand) + jiě (解 understand) = lǐjiě (理解 understand)
liàng (谅 forgive) + jiě (解 understand) = liàng jiě (谅解 pardon; forgive)
jiàn (见 view; see) + jiě (解 understand) = jiàn jiě (见解 thinking; opinion)
wù (误 mistake) + jiě (解 understand) = wù jiě (误解 misunderstand)

文 wén

1. essay; document

2. culture; civilization

3. language; literature

4. gentle; elegant

考试热词 HOT WORDS FOR TESTS

lùn (论 discuss) + wén (文 essay) = lùn wén (论文 thesis; paper)

sǎn (散 scattered) + wén (文 essay) = sǎn wén (散文 prose; essay)

zuò (作 create) + wén (文 essay) = zuò wén (作文 composition)

wén (文 essay) + zhāng (章 chapter) = wén zhāng (文章 essay)

wén (文 document) + jiàn (件 piece) = wén jiàn (文件 document)

wén (文 document) + píng (凭 evidence) = wén píng (文凭 diploma)

wén (文 document) + xiàn (献 dedicate) = wén xiàn (文献 literature; document)

wén (文 document) + jù (具 tool) = wén jù (文具 stationery)

wén (文 civilization) + huà (化 become; -ize) = wén huà (文化 culture)

wén (文 civilization) + míng (明 brightness) = wén míng (文明 civilization)

wén (文 civilization) + wù (物 things; objects) = wén wù (文物 antique; cultural relics)

wén (文 literature) + xué (学 subject; study) = wén xué (文学 literature)

wén (文 literature) + yì (艺 art) = wén yì (文艺 literature and art)

zhōng (中 China) + wén (文 language) = zhōng wén (中文 Chinese language)

wén (文 language) + zì (字 word; letter) = wén zì (文字 character; letter)

sī (斯 gentle) + wén (文 gentle) = sī wén (斯文 gentle; refined)

wén (文 gentle) + yǎ (雅 grace) = wén yǎ (文雅 elegant; grace)

Summary

Unexpected Shortcut

In this book, we discussed some basic knowledge about how the Chinese language built its vocabulary system. I hope that, you were not bored nor confused by the material.

First, we discussed the Combining Method, by which people can create unlimited words with limited characters.

Next, we discussed the three basic types of meaning-generating, which are: Coincidental Type, Opposite Type, and Integrated Type. It is quite easy to memorize them as long as you can recite a sentence as:

Xìjié juédìng chéngbài。

细节决定成败。

Details determine success or failure.

(or "The devil is in the details.")

The meanings of the above three words are generated in three different ways:

xì (细 thin) + jié (节 section) = xì jié (细节 detail) -- in the Integrated Type (T-3)

jué (决 decide) + dìng (定 decide) = jué dìng (决定 decide) - in the Coincidental Type (T-1)

chéng (成 win; success) + bài (败 fail; failure) = chéng bài (成败 success or failure; stand or fall) - in the Opposite Type (T-2)

In an exhibition area of car store, a picture shows the connection between the design and the physical product.

We also discussed three basic principles for the combining method. The principle of "Rationality" guarantees the close connections between words and our real lives. The principle of "Core-in-End" sets up a universal order in creating words, and the principle of "One-Off Function" makes it much more easier to create some complicated words, like complex words or phrases.

However, what has been discussed in this book only covers the most basic elements of the vocabulary system. A vocabulary system of any language is like the Amazon rainforest, in which there lots of unique and unusual things. For learners, especially beginners, it would be better to focus on some common and universal things.

No matter if you have realized it or not, you are already stepping into a shortcut in the forest of Chinese language. In your future learning, you will find the things we've discussed such like the thinking ways, principles, and methods are also widely applied in building up the entire language system. In other words, you already know the "Law of Jungle", which will help you to make rapid and easy progress beyond your imagination.

Quick Index of the Concepts and Terms

(listed according to the Appearing Sequence in the book)

Chinese language (Hàn yǔ 汉语)

-- A general concept for all dialects spoken by the Han Ethnicities. It also means "Mandarin Chinese" in language education. -In Section 001

Chinese language (Zhōng wén 中文)

-- Same to Hàn yǔ (汉语) -In Section 001

Mandarin Chinese (Pǔ tōng huà 普通话)

The official language of China, which is developed based on the dialects near Beijing. -In Section 001

Phonetic language (Biǎo yīn yǔ yán 表音语言)

-- A major type of language, and the essential feature is to use phonetic letters to record the meanings to build words. -In Section 002

Ideographic language (Biǎo yì yǔ yán 表意语言)

-- A major type of language, and the essential feature is to use character symbols to record the meanings to build words. -In Section 002

Word (Cí 词)

---"Words" are the most basic elements in any language, which usually have three key essential features. -In Section 003

Origin word (Yuán cí 源词)

---It specifically refers to a word that is built up only by one character. Almost all the Chinese characters are origin words. -In Section 003

Combining Method (Zǔ hé fāng fǎ 组合方法)

---It is the essential method in the Chinese language to create words by combining independent origin words. -In Section 005

Coincidental Type (Xiāng hé xíng 相合型) (T-1)

---A meaning-generating type in a combining course, in which two words with the same (or almost same) meaning are combined to make a word with the same meaning. -In Section 006

Opposite Type (xiāng chì xíng 相斥型) (T-2)

---A meaning-generating type in a combining course, in which two words with the opposite (or almost opposite) meaning are combined to make a word that refers to a general concept related to the original meanings. -In Section 006

Integrated Type (Xiāng róng xíng 相融型) (T-3)

---A meaning-generating type in a combining course, in which two origin words with different meanings are combined to make a word with an integrated meaning.-In Section 006

Principle of Rationality (Hé lǐ xìng yuán zé, 合理性原则)

---This principle means that any combining course should be based on rational logics and common knowledge. -In Section 007

Principle of Core-in-End (Hé xīn zài hòu yuán zé 核心在后原则)

---This principle means that in the combining courses based on T-3, in case there is an obvious core word, the core word should always be put at the end of the combination.-In Section 008

Principle of One-off Functioning (Yí cì xìng yuán zé 一次性原则)

---This principle means that after a combining course, each of the origin words will lose its original meaning and function.-In Section 009

Basic Words (Jī běn cí 基本词)

---Basic words are created to correspond to the elementary objects and concepts in our everyday lives. These words are listed as independent terms in dictionaries. -In Section 010

Complex Words (Fù hé cí 复合词)

---Complex words are created to describe objects and concepts with more specific features. In most cases, a complex word is created by the combination of basic words. -In Section 010

Phrase (Duǎn yǔ 短语)

---Phrases is a specific type of complex words with complicated structures and meanings. -In Section 010

About Xiaogeng's Grammar Series

Believe me when I say that millions of Mandarin Chinese learners all over the world have realized that it will bring them more surprises and personal chances if they can grasp this language well.

Even though many people believe that Chinese language is difficult to learn, the truth is that the Chinese language is not a "difficult" language but a "different" one.

One of the best ways to make things easier to learn the language is to explain the "Whys" behind the language, that is to say, to understand the thinking, reasons for principles, and the rules. These are the preconditions for knowing how to understand the language easily and to use it easily. That is the target of Xiaogeng's Grammar Series.

This series books also tries to make the learning of the Chinese language more interesting. You will never encounter obscure jargons, nor will you be frustrated by any complex theories or dizzying formulas. On the contrary, you will find that all knowledge is nothing but common sense.

A Letter to Readers

Dear Readers,

First, thank you for your interest in this wordbook, and thank you for buying it.

It is said that Pisces loved chasing dreams, and this description fits me well.

My dream is to make the Chinese language easier for learners from all over the world. I believe that the value of this dream is that it can help numerous people save time and effort so that they can put more energy into pursuing their own dreams.

I want to do things better in the future, so I hope you can do something for me: leave me your comments, suggestions, and even sharp criticism. Also, like all of the authors, I love star ratings.

If there are any suggestions, please don't hesitate to write me an email: zhouxiaogeng@163.com.

Best!

Zhou

Printed in Poland
by Amazon Fulfillment
Poland Sp. z o.o., Wrocław